COACHING
TO WIN

COACHING TO WIN

A Proven System for Developing People and Driving Performance

JANE PIERCE

OPEN BOOK
EDITIONS
A Berrett-Koehler Partner

iUniverse®

COACHING TO WIN
A PROVEN SYSTEM FOR DEVELOPING PEOPLE
AND DRIVING PERFORMANCE

iUniverse books may be ordered through booksellers or by contacting:

iUniverse
1663 Liberty Drive
Bloomington, IN 47403
www.iuniverse.com
1-800-Authors (1-800-288-4677)

ISBN: 978-1-4917-6277-6 (sc)
ISBN: 978-1-4917-6278-3 (e)

Print information available on the last page.

iUniverse rev. date: 4/8/2015

*To all the Sams—both across this country
and around the world—that I've been privileged to
work with. You are my truest teachers, and it is
your courage and determination that
inspired the writing of this book.*

CONTENTS

Foreword.. ix

Introduction xi

Chapter 1: **Sam's Dilemma**.. 1

Chapter 2: **A Breakfast Proposal** 13

Chapter 3: **Looking Deeper**.. 21

Chapter 4: **Basic Training** 36

Chapter 5: **Diving In** 48

Chapter 6: **Ironing Things Out**.. 59

Chapter 7: **The Upset** 70

Chapter 8: **The Uptick** 83

Chapter 9: **The 100 Percent Solution**...................................... 98

Chapter 10: **Victory Lap** 109

Epilogue 117

Acknowledgments... 119

About the Author 121

FOREWORD

Half-truths, misconceptions, and missteps. When it comes to leading, managers often succumb to them and companies perpetuate them.

The half-truths are that leadership is about getting things done and delivering results. The misconception is that, like the great athletic coaches, leaders devise the game plan, drill it into the team, and hold people accountable for execution.

The full truth is that leadership is about getting things done and delivering results by enabling others to be their best. A more appropriate image of coaching may come not from the ball field but from the classroom—those great teachers we've all had in grade school. They see the promise in each student, envision the oak that acorn could become, convey and uphold those high expectations, and figure out how to engage each student to grow—to figure things out on his or her own.

The work of leadership, therefore, is different from what we typically assume. It is about unleashing others' potential, helping them discover possibilities in themselves that they themselves might not even see, and tapping their capacity to get done what needs doing to deliver exceptional performance.

Jane Pierce's book takes us into the heart of this work that leaders must do but all too often overlook, postpone, or discount. Pierce puts us in the shoes of a manager who painfully discovers what he hasn't been doing, an omission that undermines his capacity to deliver results and stunts his own forward progress. Pierce then guides us to grasp the simple but hard steps of leading through coaching. As we walk in that manager's shoes, we get to try out those steps as well. Like Sam the manager, we see how we can truly get more done and deliver better results by mastering a different type of work—the work of coaching.

In an era when it is increasingly difficult to find the best talent, and at a time when a host of demographic differences—generational, national, racial, ethnic, gender—characterize our workplaces, organizations need to meet their best talent where they are and allow them to bring their all. How do you do that? Coaching. But few of us are naturals when it comes to coaching, and most of us labor under mistaken stereotypes of what coaching really entails. This book will give you a quick but powerful way of internalizing and applying a model of coaching that will bring results and transform how others experience you as a leader. Give it a try.

—Joshua D. Margolis
James Dinan and Elizabeth Miller Professor of Business Administration
Harvard Business School, December 2014

INTRODUCTION

There's one word I hear used a lot in business today: *talent*. People talk about talent as if it were the one thing that matters most. And if that were true, the formula for success would be simple. Hire top talent, and the business will prosper. However, most of us know better. We've seen, time and time again, workplaces where talent is abundant but success is still elusive.

Make no mistake. Talent is important. But if talent is never unleashed or remains underdeveloped, satisfaction and prosperity for those individuals and the company won't materialize.

When I teach leaders how to be great coaches, I often tell a story about the legendary industrialist Andrew Carnegie. Even if it's apocryphal (which is likely), it demonstrates how coaching can make a huge difference in the success of an organization by tapping into hidden talent so prevalent in today's companies.

As I tell this story, I often find I have to take a deep breath to calm my own emotions. I have seen so many times how leaders are literally transformed when they learn how to inspire others. When they apply the techniques in *Coaching to Win*, they change their relationships with their direct reports. In many cases, they begin enjoying work again, as do those who work for them. This transformation feeds my passion for teaching leaders how to coach for results.

The story goes that a journalist became interested in doing a piece on Carnegie after hearing that he had more millionaires working for him than any other company in the world. Finally getting an audience with the famous entrepreneur, the journalist asked Carnegie how he managed to persuade all these millionaires to come and work for him. Carnegie's response was surprising. "I have never recruited a single millionaire to come work for me," he said.

The journalist was intrigued. Thinking perhaps he had an even better story on his hands, he asked, "Okay then, how did you create all these millionaires you've got working for you?"

Carnegie was thoughtful for a moment and then replied, "Being a leader is much like being a prospector. You know there's gold in there, but you'll have to move a ton of dirt to find it. Too many leaders act like they're just looking for the dirt. Instead, they should be moving the dirt to find the gold in their people."

With a simple analogy, Carnegie had described the coaching formula to which he owed much of his success. I'd also add another trait of those I consider to be true leaders: when they find that gold, they give it back to their people in the form of feedback. They say, "Look how you've contributed." The effect is powerful. It raises that person's sense of his or her own value and increases the desire to contribute even more.

That's the essence of *Coaching to Win*. It's giving leaders skills that enable them to raise their colleagues' sense of value and then encouraging these same colleagues to give that value back to the company. If all this is beginning to sound a little fluffy or esoteric, it's not. The success of your business depends on it. In fact, an extensive Bersin by Deloitte study revealed that companies who truly coached their employees experienced a 21 percent uptick in business. Those are bottom-line results. So it isn't just good for people. Effective coaching is ultimately good for business.

The Bersin study also revealed another important truth. Among the companies surveyed, though leaders generally were expected to coach the people who reported to them, these leaders were found to lack the skills necessary to be effective coaches. *Coaching to Win* was designed to fill the gap—so leaders can gain coaching skills and fulfill that expectation for the good of their direct reports, themselves, and the company.

In this book, you'll meet a guy I call Sam. I wanted to wrap the lessons contained in *Coaching to Win* around a fictional character who I believe is truly relatable. I've known a lot of Sams during my years of consulting and am often struck by the commonality of their problems and the solutions to those problems. Sam's journey requires him to take an honest look at his own leadership style and to be open to a new way of going forward. Armed with that willingness and proven *Coaching to Win* techniques, Sam succeeds in writing his own happy ending.

Today, the battle is won when leaders succeed in engaging the hearts and minds of workers, not merely their hands. When hearts and minds are won, the game changes. Workers are willing to go to the mat to help the company succeed—not from fear or obligation but because their leader has ignited their own greatness. Sam is one such leader. His story demonstrates how *Coaching to Win* can become a win-win for all.

—Jane Pierce, June 2014

Chapter One
SAM'S DILEMMA

Friday, 6:46 p.m.

When he dreamed about retirement, Sam had imagined that one day he'd leave this company with his flags flying high. Retirement would be the exclamation point at the end of his career. But tonight, Sam wasn't feeling any of that. As he climbed into his car, he loosened his belt buckle. He had to do something about this weight, which was just one more thing to stress about.

He glanced at his reflection in the rearview mirror. The man he saw looking back at him was definitely not riding the waves of success. He looked absolutely drained. As he drove home from work, fighting Friday night traffic, he wondered if he could even make it through the next couple of weeks, let alone until retirement. Staring at the endless taillights in front of him, he ruminated over the tough week that had just ended and decisions that loomed in the week ahead.

First had come the news that his team had missed their targets for the third straight quarter. But that was nothing compared to what had happened next. Jerry, one of the warehouse supervisors and a star performer, walked into Sam's office just as Sam was wrapping up the day. When Sam saw him coming, he grabbed the report, thinking surely Jerry could help him come up with ideas to boost the fulfillment numbers.

But something was off. Jerry wasn't his usual lighthearted self. In fact, he looked nervous. Trying to lighten the moment, Sam said,

"What's up—worried about the game tonight? Afraid your team is going to lose?"

That's all it took. Jerry blurted it right out. He had gotten another job offer, and he'd accepted it.

Jerry went on to explain that there were several reasons why he'd taken it. The offer was one he couldn't refuse. It was more money, a shorter commute, and better hours. And then, as quickly as Jerry had come in, he left.

As Sam sat in stunned silence, he wondered if there was more to it. Over the past six months, he'd been pushing Jerry harder than usual. The warehouse wasn't making its numbers, and Jerry was the only one he could rely on to get the work out. The other supervisors just didn't seem to have the drive anymore, unable to light a fire under their teams so they'd accomplish what had to get done. Jerry did. Jerry was Sam's go-to guy, the one man who could always pull a rabbit out of his hat.

But now Jerry was leaving. Sam worried about how he would manage without him. And in the back of his mind, Sam couldn't help wondering if Jerry was leaving because of him. Sam was familiar with the saying, "People don't quit the company; they quit their boss." In Jerry's case, was that true? Sam had planned on giving him a raise when it was review time, but what did that matter now? Jerry was also the only one on the team who could have stepped into Sam's job when he retired in four years. Now what was he going to do? With Jerry gone, Sam was left with a broken, unmotivated team.

Thankfully, Jerry had given two weeks' notice. That would buy a little time to find a replacement. But who? How could he replace someone like Jerry?

Tiny raindrops spattered the windshield. Sam flicked his wipers on slow speed. It hadn't always been like this. He remembered joining the company straight out of school. He'd had big dreams about his career back then and soon realized that he'd need a degree to make those dreams come true. So as soon as he was eligible for the company's tuition reimbursement program, Sam had enrolled part time at the local college. Six and a half years later, he had his degree in supply-chain management and his first promotion. He was on his way.

Twenty-five years and several promotions later, Sam's dream had become a reality. He was made manager of the largest parts warehouse in the company.

The raindrops were getting larger, and with them Sam faced a growing realization. Instead of spending his last years with the company reveling in his accomplishments, he was drearily counting down the days to retirement. Not exactly what he'd planned.

It was pouring hard by the time Sam pulled into the driveway. The battery in his garage door opener chose today to go dead, forcing him to make a mad dash through the rain to the front door. Sam stood dripping in the foyer for a moment, catching his breath. He listened. The house was empty. He knew he was late. The traffic jam had been unrelenting. But he'd avoided the accident that had fouled up everyone's Friday night commute, and that was some consolation. He found a note on the table from his wife, telling him she was out running errands and that he'd find his dinner in the oven.

Sam grabbed his dinner and a Heineken from the fridge and headed for the patio. The rain had stopped, but a bank of dark clouds to the west still threatened. He poked at the food, not really hungry. Pushing the plate aside and taking a long sip from the green bottle, he contemplated what to do about Jerry. As much as he tried to focus on a solution, he couldn't avoid going back to that nagging question: "Is Jerry quitting me?"

Sam recalled some of the managers he'd had in his past. Some were real pieces of work. The last guy he'd reported to was a complete jerk, a yeller who constantly told people they were idiots. Sam had promised himself that when he became manager, he would never treat people that way. And when he did get the promotion, he tried hard to be one of the guys.

But in time, some of his team had begun taking advantage of Sam's easygoing spirit. Performance numbers started to slip, so he had to get a little tougher. But at his very worst, he was nothing like the prior manager. Of that he was sure. He got frustrated at times, and occasionally he lost his temper, but didn't everyone? The warehouse could be a pressure cooker sometimes. He always went back and made amends once he'd calmed down. The truth was, sometimes he had to lay down the law to get the guys in gear.

Sam admitted he was at a total loss for what to do. And without food, the beer was going straight to his head. He couldn't concentrate. He grabbed his untouched plate and the empty beer bottle and headed inside as the second wave of rain began to pound the deck.

Gloom hung over Sam for the remainder of the weekend. On Monday morning, he dragged himself into the office. No sooner had he sat down and started going through his e-mail when he heard a tap on his door. Looking up from the monitor, he saw Reggie leaning in his doorway. Reggie was Sam's boss, the regional manager. *This is all I need today,* Sam thought, convinced that Reggie had arrived to grill him about his lackluster production numbers.

He was wrong. Reggie came in and sat opposite him. His manner was surprisingly pleasant for someone who was about take Sam to task for another period of poor results. "How are you doing?" Reggie asked genuinely. "I heard the news about Jerry and wanted to come talk to you about your plans for filling his position."

Sam was amazed. How had Reggie heard about Jerry? Who else knew? Was Sam the last to know?

Sighing, Sam replied, "Yeah, Jerry's announcement came as a real shocker. He dropped it on me Friday night." Trying to be upbeat, Sam continued, "He's giving us a two-week notice, so I need to get the job posted right away."

Reggie eyed him.

"Honestly, I'm a little concerned that it's going to take a lot longer than two weeks to fill those shoes," Sam confessed. "Jerry was my best guy."

Reggie was thoughtful. "Do you have anyone else on the crew who can be moved over?" he asked.

Sam hesitated to answer, not wanting to admit he didn't have anyone in mind. Grooming folks to fill future positions was a big thing to Reggie. Sam had always planned to do it, but the production numbers had taken most of his attention. He'd had the best intentions, but now the worm had turned. He had no one to blame but himself.

Sam felt trapped. There never seemed to be enough time to get everything done no matter how many hours he worked. He pushed back against the feeling of being overwhelmed. He still had time. The best laid plans, he thought. He hadn't planned on retiring for another four years, and by then Jerry would have been ready to move up to the role of manager. He'd never imagined that Jerry wouldn't be there, that the man would just up and quit. Now there was a huge gap in his team and no one to fill it.

But Reggie had asked a direct question, and it required a straight answer. Finally, he told Reggie, "No, I don't have anyone who is close to being ready. I'll probably have to go outside to fill the job."

Reggie was quiet for a while. When a few moments had passed, he leaned forward in his chair and asked, "What's going on, Sam?"

Sam, dumbfounded, was unsure how to respond. He felt a thin layer of sweat rising on the back of his neck. Was Reggie kidding? Wasn't it obvious what was "going on"? Sam wasn't hitting his numbers, he'd lost his best guy, and he'd just had to admit to his regional manager that he hadn't been successful in developing his people—one of Reggie's top priorities. Sam had never looked like a bigger failure. He knew it, and now his boss knew it too.

Reggie's question hung in the stuffy air. Sam's office sat at the top of the stairs on the second floor. It was his habit to keep the blinds open so that he had an unobstructed view of the activity on the warehouse floor. Although Reggie had closed the door after coming in, people walking past could glance through the glass and see the two men locked in conversation.

Before Sam could offer anything in his own defense, Reggie spoke again. "Sam," he said, "What I really want to say is I realize that I haven't been a very good leader. I want to apologize."

Sam couldn't believe his ears. He was glad that Reggie wasn't reprimanding him, but what was he talking about? Reggie was a great leader. In fact, Sam tried to imitate Reggie more than any manager he'd ever known. "Are you kidding me?" Sam blurted. "You don't have anything to apologize for. I should apologize for letting you down. You were the one who really pushed to get me this job, and look how I've paid you back. Our numbers are down, and I just lost the one guy who had any potential. And to top it all off, I have no clue how to turn this around besides posting Jerry's job, crossing my fingers, and hoping for the best. I've been wracking my brain all weekend long, and that's the best I can give you. I'm afraid things are going to get worse here before they get better."

"Perhaps," Reggie answered, but he didn't seem to share Sam's worst-case prognosis. "I'm going to work with you on turning this around," he said. "I feel responsible because I failed to give you the training and support you needed when you took this job."

Sam was about to object, but he let it ride. Besides, Reggie didn't seem as troubled by his own failure as Sam was by his.

Reggie continued, "I have some other appointments this morning, but let's block out time this afternoon to work on a strategy together. I'll be back here at two." He rose to go, but before he opened the office door, he turned back to Sam, smiled, and said, "Oh, and Sam? Chin up. It's not the end of the world. You're going to land on your feet, and I'll be right there with you. See you in a couple hours."

Sam leaned back in his chair and watched his boss disappear down the hallway. In the fifteen minutes since Reggie had walked in, his whole world had done a 180. Nothing had been solved. In fact, nothing had changed at all. He still had to fill Jerry's job and figure out how to improve his production numbers with one less person on the team. What had changed is that he no longer felt alone.

He tackled his calendar and quickly reorganized his day to free up the afternoon. He definitely wanted to be focused when Reggie came back.

The morning blew by. Sam contacted HR, working with Sarah to pull the warehouse superintendent job description and get it posted. He then called together his other three warehouse supervisors and talked about how they would cover Jerry's team until a replacement could be found. They'd all known Jerry was leaving. It seemed like everyone knew Jerry was leaving. Again, Sam wondered if he'd been the last to know. But he couldn't let that distract him. Right now, his priority was getting his remaining guys to take on the extra work necessary to hit the numbers and cover Jerry's team.

To say they were less than enthusiastic would have been an understatement. He could hear them grumbling as they filed out of his office. *What's wrong with employees today?* Sam wondered. In his earlier years, Sam would have seen this challenge as an opportunity to really shine, to stand out. Not these guys. They seemed put out that they had to work a little harder for the company, and especially for Sam. He also worried about pushing them too hard. What if more people quit? What would he do then?

At exactly 2:00 p.m., Reggie was back in Sam's office. "What's going on?" asked Reggie.

Sam jumped in his seat, startled. He hadn't even heard Reggie come in. Wanting to seem like he was now on top of things, Sam said, "I met with my guys on how we're going to cover things until Jerry's replacement can be found." His frustration was evident as he went on, "They didn't seem too thrilled to be taking on the extra workload."

Reggie let out a soft "Hmm."

Sam continued in damage-control mode. "I did contact HR today. They'll post the job listing internally for three days and then expand the search outside the company." He desperately wanted Reggie to see that he had this under control. But he wondered why he'd told Reggie about the negative reaction from his team. If he was trying to make it look like he was back in charge, adding that unfortunate detail didn't help his case.

If Reggie was annoyed, he didn't show it. "Great," he said. "Getting the job posted is priority number one. But that's the easy part." Sam wondered what was coming next. Reggie said, "Tell me about how you shared the news with your guys and specifically what their response was."

So the two men spent time talking about how Sam had presented the information to his three warehouse supervisors. They discussed the fact that Sam had not invited Jerry to the meeting. Sam tried to explain his rationale. Jerry had already decided he was leaving. He'd given his notice. Therefore, Jerry was no longer key to the discussion.

Reggie leaned back in his chair. "Sam, this is where we need to begin. Let's think about how that meeting could have gone a little differently."

Sam stiffened at Reggie's criticism.

"For any of this to work," Reggie said, "you'll need to agree to be open to my coaching and not get defensive, okay? I'm not trying to put the blame on you or anyone else."

With that, Sam relaxed a little.

"I want to use this meeting with your guys as a learning opportunity," Reggie went on. "You're going to have a lot more meetings with your guys. There are things that could be done a little differently that will make those future meetings more successful. My only objective is to set you up for success going forward. Are you up for this?"

Sam still felt defensive, but replied, "I guess. Let's give it a shot."

Reggie smiled. "Okay. Let's start with not including Jerry in your meeting this morning. What made you not invite him?"

"Well," said Sam, "I know this team has to hold it together without Jerry, so it made sense to me to have them begin now." But Sam knew the real reason: he resented Jerry for resigning and didn't want to deal with him. If Jerry hadn't quit, all Sam would have had to worry about right now was the production numbers.

"Your reasoning makes sense on the surface," Reggie responded, "but remember that these guys have worked with Jerry for years. They've become friends. Because of your exclusion of Jerry, your guys probably came in with a negative attitude in the first place."

Reggie was right. Sam recalled the way the meeting had started. Two of his guys had been sitting in chairs, leaning back with their arms crossed. The other one had been standing off to the side, and his arms had been crossed too. Everything about their body language and facial expressions should have signaled that there was a problem, but Sam had been so focused on getting the meeting done before he met with Reggie, he hadn't taken time to notice the signs.

Reggie was moving on. "How did the rest of the meeting go?"

"Pretty well, considering." But now Sam was beginning to wonder himself. "I told the guys how we were going to divide the work, and who'd be responsible for what. I tried to be really clear and make sure the workload got divided evenly. Then they went back to work."

"There was no discussion?" asked Reggie. "Did you get their ideas? Ask for their opinions?"

"They didn't say anything," Sam said, now recognizing his mistake. "They just nodded and went back to work." He thought about how the guys had left the room. Nick had shoved the table slightly when he stood up. Sam hadn't thought it was on purpose, but now he wondered if it meant something.

Reggie kept going. "Based on what you've shared with me so far, I'd like to play it back to you from their point of view. Is that okay?"

Sam nodded.

"You call your three warehouse supervisors into a meeting. You don't invite Jerry. It probably makes them feel uncomfortable. Remember, these guys are friends. They've been loyal to each other. So now they come in feeling like they have to choose between being loyal to the company and being loyal to their friend."

Sam listened. This was hard for him to hear, but he knew Reggie was right.

"I'm not sure if you acknowledged Jerry's contributions to the company, or if you just got to the business at hand; I wasn't there. However, if you jumped right into dividing up the work without acknowledging Jerry, they most likely thought you saw all of them as disposable assets too. Put yourself in their shoes. They're probably thinking, 'Would he really care, beyond the inconvenience, if any of us left? He'd just divide the work among the remaining folks and move on.'"

Sam was silent. He was trying to see it from his warehouse supervisors' perspective, but it was hard. He had a warehouse to run, and he didn't have a lot of time to hold hands or worry about feelings. But he could see where Reggie was coming from.

Feeling Sam's silence, Reggie asked, "How did you engage the guys in dividing the workload?"

"I asked them if they had any questions," Sam replied defensively, "but they didn't say anything."

"I get it," said Reggie. He paused, adjusting his approach. After a moment, he began again. "Look, when I started out as a manager, I would have conducted the meeting exactly the way you did." Sam felt a little relieved. "But I've learned some techniques that have helped me grow as a leader. I don't for a moment doubt that your intentions were good. All I want to do is share with you what I learned and help you be more effective in your role as a leader. You all right with that?"

"Sure," said Sam, but the satisfaction he'd felt just before this meeting was gone. Had he done anything right? It didn't feel like it.

Reggie was ready to move on. "Let me leave you with something to think about tonight," he told Sam. "Ask yourself how you might have run that meeting differently if you had focused on this saying:

People are more likely to support that which they help create.

"Think about it, and let's meet for breakfast tomorrow morning at the Downtown Café. I'm anxious to hear what you come up with. I'll also have some more ideas to share with you then."

As Reggie left, Sam quickly wrote down the saying on a yellow pad and stuffed it in his bag. By tomorrow morning, his boss expected an answer to what he might have done differently in the meeting, and he was going to deliver.

Sam repeated the phrase in his head: *People are more likely to support that which they help create.* He started thinking about the last part of the sentence. *Well, I guess I didn't have them help create anything. I came up with the plan and told them what to do. But after all, isn't that what a manager does? Isn't it up to me to come up with the solution, clearly tell them what they need to do, and then get out of their way and let them do it?*

Sam rubbed the back of his neck, confused. Everything Reggie had said made sense in theory, but how about when the rubber met the road? There, he wasn't so sure. Still, he resolved to give it a try. He thought, *Okay. I need to have an answer for tomorrow morning. So maybe, for the sake of argument, I should look at this differently.* And he began to wonder how he could have let the warehouse supervisors create part of the solution.

Sam mulled that question over as he drove home. The sky was mostly overcast, with occasional patches of blue breaking through the gray clouds. And the traffic was lighter tonight. No accidents, thank goodness. Reaching home, Sam kissed his wife, grabbed a quick shower, and then joined her at the dinner table. They had their usual conversation, but Sam's mind kept drifting to Reggie's question. He ended up leaving half the food on his plate. Together, he and his wife cleaned up the kitchen.

Sam spent the next two hours in an easy chair with his yellow pad, but by bedtime, he was no closer to an answer. In less than eight hours, he'd be meeting Reggie over breakfast, and he had nothing. Sam saw his trouble: he'd never worked for anyone who let him help create anything. Each manager throughout his career had simply told him what to do. And he had done it. This would require a whole new way of thinking, and Sam was growing more convinced he really wasn't up to it.

Unable to sleep, Sam rolled around in bed for what seemed like hours. Finally, exhausted, he drifted off to sleep around three o'clock in the morning. In a dream, he found himself sitting behind his desk. His three warehouse supervisors walked in for the meeting. Nick and Mike plopped down in chairs, leaning back with arms crossed. Craig was standing off to the side, also with arms crossed.

"Look, I know this is tough," Sam addressed the three. "Jerry's one of us, and now he's leaving."

Nick grumbled, "If Jerry's one of us, why isn't he in this meeting? He's not gone yet, and you shouldn't treat him like he is!"

The outburst surprised Sam. Nick had always been a quiet, easygoing guy. "Nick," Sam said in an even tone, "this meeting is about how we're going to keep it together after Jerry leaves. If you guys think it would be better to do that with Jerry in the room, let's get him in here."

Sam eyed the room, noticing that the body language had started to shift. Craig, who'd been standing in the corner away from the group, took a seat. Nick and Mike leaned forward in their chairs and uncrossed their arms. Sam picked up the phone and paged Jerry. Soon Jerry buzzed in, and Sam asked him to join the meeting.

When Jerry arrived, Sam started the meeting again. "Okay, everyone knows that Jerry is moving on to his next great adventure. He's done an outstanding job for us, and we're really going to miss him. We need to keep this place running until we've found and trained Jerry's replacement. I need your help coming up with a plan so that we can cover the work and hit our numbers. Does anybody have any ideas?"

The question was like magic. It no sooner left Sam's mouth than ideas from the team began to fill the room. So many, in fact, that Sam had a tough time writing them all down. He asked the guys to take on the challenge and return by the end of the day with a plan. No grumbling as they left this time. When they walked out of the room now, they sounded like true warehouse supervisors.

Sam glanced at his watch. Having gotten the team into action, he now had the rest of the afternoon to focus on the numbers.

Sam woke up smiling, a full ten minutes before the alarm. Quickly he wrote down the particulars, showered, and prepared for his breakfast with Reggie. Sam couldn't predict exactly how the meeting with his boss would go. He did know one thing, however. He already had one heck of an appetite.

Chapter Two
A BREAKFAST PROPOSAL

Tuesday, 7:15 a.m.

His enthusiasm was still running high as Sam drove toward the Downtown Café for his breakfast meeting with Reggie. He couldn't wait to tell Reggie what he'd come up with. Sam was still a little mystified by the dream and the clarity of the answers it provided. He was grateful that he now had a plan—wherever it came from—but he'd keep the dream part to himself. No need for that to get around the warehouse. He had to admit, though, that something new was happening. For an old dog that had learned all the tricks, he was beginning to see new possibilities. He felt like he owed it to Reggie, his team, and himself to stay open to them.

A slice of sunshine was peeking out from the large gray cloud directly ahead. Sam's mind went to next steps. He imagined calling his supervisors together again, including Jerry this time, and taking another run at the meeting. After all, they'd just met yesterday. His guys wouldn't have had time to implement any of the changes yet. It seemed right. That way he could try out Reggie's idea of allowing them to help create the change.

Sam lucked out finding a parking spot on North Main, right in front of the restaurant. Walking through the front door, he spied Reggie already seated at a booth in the corner.

"Hey, Sam!" The greeting was cordial, yet Reggie seemed a little preoccupied. "I'm a little early, but something's come up and I have to leave in half an hour." A waitress approached the table and both men quickly ordered—the café scramble for Reggie, while Sam got his usual hotcakes and sausage. Coffee cups were filled and the waitress left the men to continue their discussion.

"So let's get started," Reggie said. "I want to make sure we have enough time for an idea I'd like to run by you. First, though, tell me what you came up with. How would you have run that meeting with your supervisors differently if you'd applied the concept?

People are more likely to support that which they help create.

Sam shifted in his seat. "Well," he began, "I'd first lay out the problem: how to cover the team until we've trained Jerry's replacement. Then I'd ask them to work together to come up with ideas and come back to me with a detailed plan."

Sam paused, trying to read what Reggie thought of this approach. The words replayed in Sam's head. It all sounded way too easy, and he felt uncomfortable. Sam had always thought it was his job to come up with solutions, and his warehouse supervisors were there to execute his plans. The approach he'd just put forward felt like he was dumping the problem on his direct reports and, in effect, abdicating his own responsibility for making the warehouse run efficiently.

While he tried to read Reggie's mind, Reggie was clearly reading his. Looking directly at Sam, Reggie quietly asked, "And what will your role be, Sam?"

Sam's confidence in his plan was wavering. This was unfamiliar territory. It didn't feel right. Clearly he'd gone too far. He tried to absorb the question.

"What do you mean?" he asked Reggie finally.

In a reassuring tone, Reggie began, "I think your idea is on the right track. My question wasn't meant to shake your confidence. I'm only asking what you'll do next. In other words, once your guys come up with a plan, how will you ensure it meets its objective so the warehouse hits its numbers and runs effectively? What's your role in the process?"

Sam thought for a moment. "I'd have to hear them out," he replied, "and then let them know if their idea would work, I guess."

Reggie was quick to add, "And you'll have to do all that in a way that won't shut them down." The waitress arrived with two steaming plates, and the men began to eat.

Between bites, Reggie went on. "By letting them help create the solution, you're not throwing up your hands and telling them to go solve the problem. You're giving them an opportunity to voice their ideas, which will be incorporated into the ultimate solution. Remember, they're the ones on the front lines every day. They're closest to the actual work. However, you're accountable for the warehouse. By solving the problem together, you create an opportunity for them to come up with the best solution, gaining their buy-in at the same time. It's a win-win for everybody."

Sam thought it over, poking the remaining sausage link with his fork. He knew Reggie was right. After a swig of coffee, he said, "That really makes sense. I was thinking about bringing the guys back together this afternoon, including Jerry, and asking for their ideas. I'm not sure what they'll come up with that'll be any different from what I asked them for yesterday, but I see now how just giving them the opportunity to think through a solution will help win their support." Sam smiled at Reggie and, with a shrug, added, "And at this point I need all the support I can get, right?"

Reggie was smiling now too. "I think that's a great idea!" he told Sam. "Let me know how it goes. Tell them from the very beginning that you really want their ideas but you reserve the right to make the final decision. That way they'll know that, although their ideas will be considered, you still have the final word."

Sam nodded in agreement.

With a glance at his watch, Reggie was ready to move on. "Now I have something else I want to discuss. Last year our company decided that coaching and feedback are keys to keeping our workforce engaged. You may remember there was a lot of communication going around about that."

Sam rewound to the previous year and replied, "Yeah, I remember something about that. But frankly, I didn't think it really applied to us. I mean, I talk to my guys every single day. We're always in touch. It seemed like it was more directed at the folks in the corporate office, rather than us guys out in the warehouse."

Reggie said, "Talking to your guys every day is great, but it may not be enough. It's not just about talking and giving orders. To be an effective coach, you need to give them feedback on how they're doing, and specifically on how their performance contributes to the company's success."

Reggie waited a moment, allowing that thought to sink in. The waitress came by again. They waved away her offer to refill their cups, and she placed a check on the corner of the table.

"Anyway," Reggie continued, "I had a chance to attend a training program called *Coaching to Win*. Frankly, Sam, at the time I wasn't sure if I'd get anything out of it. And I had plenty to keep me busy. But I'm sure glad I did it. It taught me a lot of new techniques on coaching and providing effective feedback. It's probably one of the best training programs I've ever gone through."

Reggie paused again. "Sam," he said, "I meant it the other day when I apologized for not coaching you effectively. If I'd been applying what I learned in *Coaching to Win* to our relationship all along, you'd have a guy to take over for Jerry."

Sam wondered what was going on. It felt like Reggie had been leading up to something; he just wasn't sure what. But he didn't have to wonder much longer. Reggie looked directly at him and said, "I want to sign you up for *Coaching to Win*. Would you be open to that?"

Sam weighed Reggie's invitation. He was trying to hide his feelings, which weren't too positive. All he could think of was the pile of work already on his plate. And now he'd have to add some training class to it? With the numbers down and the challenge of replacing Jerry still looming, how could he make time for this? Had Reggie completely forgotten that Sam had just lost his best guy and was scrambling to figure out how to get everything done with one less person?

A lot was going through his mind. He could already feel the stress of interviewing dozens of people to find Jerry's replacement. And, to top it all off, now he couldn't just tell his guys what to do anymore. Reggie wanted him to start asking them to come up with their own ideas on how to solve the work distribution issue.

Right now, *Coaching to Win* felt like the straw that might finally break Sam's back. *I don't have time for this* ran through his mind like a mantra. But Reggie was his boss; refusing really was not an option.

The half hour was up. Snatching the check, Reggie tried not to look impatient as he waited for Sam's response. Sam was growing impatient too, wondering how many fires were already blazing back at the warehouse. Staring at the uneaten sausage on his plate, Sam said the only thing he felt a guy in his position could say: "Sure—sign me up."

Hanging a right on Garfield, Sam headed for the warehouse, making a brave attempt to talk himself down from his tree. Nothing would happen right away, he told himself. It would be at least a couple of months before the next *Coaching to Win* workshop was even available. He knew a lot of the company leaders were doing this same training and would definitely be in the queue ahead of him. In Sam's best-case scenario, he'd have enough time to get through his current issues before he'd even have to worry about it.

For now, he'd take things one step at a time. His first e-mail of the day went to his warehouse supervisors, inviting them to get together that afternoon and talk further about how they were going to cover the team until Jerry's replacement was hired. As promised, he also invited Jerry. Sam was again skeptical that they'd come up with ideas that were any better than his own. After all, he'd been around a lot longer than any of these guys. He'd also been one of them not all that long ago. He knew what he was doing. Still, he'd told Reggie he would try the new approach with them, and he intended to keep his word.

Feeling relieved, Sam hit Send and started going through his other e-mails. He scrolled quickly through the column of almost forty new messages, scanning their subject lines. One in particular caught his eye—a calendar invitation from the company's training department.

Invitation

Corporate Training

To: Sam Wainwright

From: Coaching to Win

cc: Reggie Dahlgren

RE: **Welcome to the *Coaching to Win* Learning Experience**

Dear Sam:

Congratulations on beginning the *Coaching to Win* learning experience! This marks the beginning of an exciting journey to enhance the knowledge, skills, and abilities that will strengthen your effectiveness as a coach.

The meeting invitation was for the following Tuesday, and it contained an attachment. Sam sighed. He'd told himself this thing wouldn't happen for another couple of months. Yeah, right—and it didn't rain in Indianapolis in the summertime. Unenthused, but remembering his commitment to Reggie, he sighed again and clicked Accept.

Sam tackled his unread e-mails—forty-seven of them to be exact—and was about to start a more in-depth analysis of the warehouse's lagging numbers for the period. Something, however, drew him back to the *Coaching to Win* invitation. He clicked the e-mail again, curious now about the attachment. Being the type who didn't like surprises, Sam decided to open it and see what it was. This move brought up something called a field guide, with a section entitled "Phase 1: Self-Discovery."

He quickly scanned through it, thinking, "Oh boy, here we go." This was clearly going to take some time—the one thing he didn't have right now. He had several issues in the warehouse that needed to be resolved before the end of the day, and then there was the meeting with Jerry and the other supervisors.

Sam had never been a guy who liked to take work home. He felt that if you applied yourself, there was no reason you couldn't get your work done at the workplace. But he feared falling behind, and now the die was cast. Like it or not, this training was starting next week. Reluctantly, he decided to print out the field guide and read it at home tonight. Right now, he needed to get out of his office and see what was going on in the warehouse.

The rest of Sam's day was quickly devoured by a variety of warehouse issues. And there was the redo of the meeting with the supervisors and Jerry. At a quarter to six, tired and a little punchy, Sam was shutting down his office.

Reaching to flick off his desk lamp, he spotted out of the corner of his eye the *Coaching to Win* field guide in his printer tray. *End to a perfect day*, he thought, and he was tempted to ignore it and keep walking out the door. Something, however, made him think better of it. Sam recalled that Reggie had been copied on the training invitation. What if Reggie called tomorrow, asking if he'd looked through the materials?

He had to stay ahead of this thing somehow. Sam grabbed the field guide from the printer and headed to his car. There was still some daylight left, but he could see a band of thunderclouds forming again to the southwest. As Garfield flowed into the parkway, he wondered if this lousy weather would ever end. His mood felt cloudy too, and he hoped on both horizons that there was some sunshine coming up soon.

Once he arrived home, the stress of the day began to dissipate. Sam enjoyed a couple of beers and a low-key dinner with his wife, Linda. After twenty-six years of marriage, their conversation was easy and relaxed, mostly about their kids and Linda's plan to remodel the kitchen. They were empty nesters now, and it was really more house than they needed. But, as they kept telling themselves, there would be grandkids eventually.

At nine thirty, Sam was already feeling sleepy. He told his wife good night and started upstairs, but he stopped when he saw the field guide on the hall table, right where he'd tossed it when he arrived home. Reaching over the bannister, he grabbed it and continued up the stairs.

Kicking off his shoes and sitting on a corner of the bed, Sam flipped through the pages. Surprisingly, the whole thing seemed less intimidating now. To be sure, this was going to take some time. But it seemed doable. It began with a bunch of questions—an assessment to find out where he was with his coaching skills. Still, it was getting late, and Sam was determined to take the time and do it right. Better after a good night's sleep, he told himself. Brushing his teeth, he caught a smile reflected in the mirror. He'd been thinking about that dream from last night. Maybe more answers would come in his sleep. Sam got into bed and closed his eyes. Tomorrow was another day.

Chapter Three

LOOKING DEEPER

Wednesday, 7:35 a.m.

Sam was up before the sun. Something in him wanted to get a jump on this *Coaching to Win* training, which was now less than a week away. Armed with fresh, hot coffee in his favorite mug, he sat down at his desk and opened the field guide. Flipping past the initial pages, he stopped on page 5, which listed the steps he'd have to complete in phase 1 of the training:

Step 1: Self-Discovery
- ❏ Complete the Behavioral Assessment.
- ❏ Complete the Coaching Skills Self-Assessment.
- ❏ Complete the questions for phase 1 in the Field Guide.

Step 2: Introductory Kick-Off Call
- ❏ Participate in the Kick-Off Conference Call.
- ❏ Identify a potential coachee (to be confirmed by your direct manager).

Step 3: Manager Meeting
- ❏ Schedule a meeting with your direct manager to
    - discuss your *Coaching to Win* learning experience and his/her expectations and
    - agree on whom you will be coaching and what you will be focusing on.

It seemed like a lot, but Sam committed to taking it one step at a time. Moving ahead to page 7, he found instructions for completing the online behavioral assessment. It looked easy enough, and the final bullet point of the instructions said it should take ten minutes, tops, to complete. That was good news. He had plenty of other things on his plate today.

Sam clicked on the link and started reading. The instructions seemed clear. He read through the various descriptions and selected the ones that fit. Still, Sam couldn't help wondering how this exercise would reveal anything meaningful about his behavior or communication style. But he had time right now and pressed on to get it done.

Then Sam went back to the field guide and started working on the coaching skills self-assessment. This assessment consisted of twenty statements. You had to rate yourself on a five-degree scale that ranged from "never" to "always." Sam tried to answer as honestly as possible. Some made him feel a little edgy. For instance, statement 3 asked him if, when working with his people, he focused on both their strengths and areas for improvement. What were they getting at? It seemed like a trick question. His guys knew their own strengths. Wasn't his job to help them improve in areas they weren't so effective? And where was he supposed to find time for all of this anyway?

Still, he tried not to second-guess himself. Deep down, Sam believed he was a good manager. But plenty of challenges were coming his way right now, and if he could up his game by learning some new coaching skills, he was all for it.

Some of the statements seemed a little esoteric too. Take statement 10: "I give feedback so that my coachee understands how his/her efforts help the company meet business goals." Maybe that's how you talked about things in a business school classroom, Sam thought. But he lived in the real world, in this warehouse. His numbers were down, and with Jerry leaving, he'd soon be shorthanded. He didn't have time for a lot of chitchat with the guys. And wasn't that statement a little obvious anyway? If his guys did their jobs and met their goals, wouldn't the company meet its goals as well? Why make things complicated?

Determined to complete the task, he finished ranking himself on all twenty statements. The field guide indicated he'd receive a report on his behavioral assessment, which he needed before he could go any further. Sam figured the report wouldn't show up for a couple of days, at least. He'd finished in a little more than twenty minutes, so chalk up one victory for today. He laid the materials aside and began focusing on the real work.

As it turned out, Sam's intuition had been spot-on. About an hour later, his phone rang. It was Reggie, calling to give Sam an encouraging nudge to begin his training assignment. With a smile, Sam told Reggie that he was already on it. "I completed both of the assessments and will finish the rest of the questions when I receive my report," he stated.

Reggie sounded pleasantly surprised. "That's great!" he exclaimed. "Based on how you reacted at breakfast, you didn't seem very excited about this training. I thought I'd have to prod you a little." They shared a laugh, and Reggie added, "I guess that shows it works both ways. By using what I learned in *Coaching to Win* with you, you were more motivated to get with the program."

After the call, Sam got to work. They'd already received a few applications for Jerry's job from folks within the company. He thumbed through the sheaf of papers. Nothing looked promising; the applicants were nice individuals who were enthusiastic but lacked either the right background or enough experience. Sam would interview them anyway, but instinct told him that to get a real hitter like Jerry, they'd have to look outside.

He swiveled in his chair and peered out the window behind his desk, which overlooked the warehouse floor. It was a busy day. Sam spotted Nick, Mike, and Craig engaged in conversation. He wondered if they were kicking around ideas for the plan. Sam thought back to the second meeting he'd had with them. He was getting better at reading body language, recalling that the guys had seemed more present and less defensive, as compared to the crossed arms he'd been up against the first time. The whole tone was different, a new energy.

He watched Nick, who was now talking enthusiastically. Of the three, Sam's money was on Nick. Nick seemed to have the most initiative. He shared a lot of Jerry's qualities but was still a little green. In a perfect world, Sam would be helping Nick become less so.

He wondered if this *Coaching to Win* stuff would really make his job easier. He knew he needed help. And after the self-assessment, Sam wondered if he was doing right by his guys. He realized he hadn't rated himself very highly on a number of those statements. Could he learn new tricks? It was a good question that didn't yet have an answer, but maybe he'd find one as the training went on.

Sam's gaze went to the bigger picture. He looked out on the warehouse. Somewhere in that vast space, there had to be clues for how to get their numbers up. In this environment, it always came down to efficiency. Find faster and better ways to do things, and the benefits would go right to the bottom line. "Process improvements" they called them. There was a time when Sam had given a lot of thought to that kind of stuff. But lately, he'd been struggling just to keep up. It was frustrating, thinking that the answers might be right under his nose if he only had time to see them.

The day dragged on. Seemed like more of the usual. No shortage of problems; solutions were what seemed scarce. Sam decided to wait until tomorrow before checking with his supervisors about their plan for covering Jerry's job. Then he decided to invite Jerry in, and they sat in Sam's office, shared a cup of coffee, and reflected on Jerry's early days at the warehouse. The interaction left both men feeling good. Sam was gradually working through his resentment about Jerry leaving. He was beginning to realize that Jerry wasn't really the problem. The problem was not having anyone ready to fill Jerry's shoes, and Sam knew the responsibility for that was ultimately his.

At eleven minutes before six, Sam decided that he'd done about all he could for that day. Taking one last scan of e-mail before powering down his computer, he was surprised to see that he'd already received a message from *Coaching to Win* that contained the report on his behavioral assessment. He was torn between his curiosity to see how he'd done and his desire to clock out after a long day. Splitting the difference, he sent the document to print, grabbed it from the printer tray, and headed out the door. *Good bedtime reading*, he thought.

The evening traffic was surprisingly light, and Sam got home a good ten minutes earlier than usual. He and Linda dined at one end of the kitchen table on leftover grilled chicken and steamed broccoli from the night before. Sam's doctor had been candid with him recently about lowering his cholesterol. Exercise was another thing he just couldn't seem to find the time for. The other end of the table was an interlocking mosaic of paint swatches, cabinet finishes, flooring samples, and appliance brochures—Linda's kitchen remodeling project.

Sam had tossed his behavioral assessment report at that end of the table too. As he and Linda talked and ate, he tried to give her his full attention. Sam knew that when retirement came, they'd be spending more time together, and he wanted to maintain good communication. Still, he felt his mind wandering to the report. His ego had been taking a few hits at work lately. He hoped there was something encouraging in that report, along with a couple of things he'd probably have to work on.

As they cleared the plates, Linda saw the report and asked Sam with a smile, "Do you have homework tonight?"

Sam hadn't told Linda anything about the *Coaching to Win* training he was about to do. He was old school, preferring to keep his work at work. But something made him want to share with her. Quickly he explained the program and the assessment he'd done that morning.

"Well, have you looked at the results?" Linda asked.

"No, honey," Sam replied. "I got them just as I was leaving."

Linda's attention migrated to her remodeling samples. Sam grabbed a Heineken out of the fridge, sat back down at the table, and opened the report.

There were twenty-three pages in all. Some of the report material was very technical, charts and graphs that presumably had scored Sam's responses and plotted them by some metric. This would take some explaining. Maybe he could ask Reggie or inquire about it during the conference call next week.

Sam read through the narrative. As he sipped his beer, he felt himself frowning, a frown that got deeper the more he read. Finished, he tossed the pages down and let out a tense sigh. Linda stopped reading and looked up. "Bad news?" she asked.

He set down his beer and looked at her directly. "Do you think I'm a bad listener?" he asked.

A moment went by. Feeling a little accused by her silence, Sam said at last, "Am I?"

Linda set down the appliance brochure, calculating her response. "Well," she began cautiously, "you listen sometimes."

Sam knew there was a "but" coming, so he waited for his wife to continue.

"Look, I'm not trying to hurt your feelings. But a lot of the time, you're moving so fast, you just want to get things done. It doesn't give others time to voice their opinions."

They eyed each other. "Mind if I take a look?" she asked finally.

Sighing, Sam slid her the report. Linda read in silence for several minutes and then put the report down. She looked at her husband and smiled.

After twenty-six years of marriage, Sam already knew what his wife was thinking. Still, with whatever optimism he could muster, he asked, "Well …?"

"Sam, you know I love you," she said. "But I think there's a lot in here that's spot-on." Her face softened, seeing his distress. She added, "That includes the positive too. You are focusing on what sounds critical and not giving yourself credit for what you are doing right. I'm no expert, but I'd guess that the purpose behind this training isn't to make you feel bad. It's to help you see where you can improve your coaching skills and give you the tools to do that."

Over the years, Sam had been reminded many times why he married the woman now sitting beside him. This was one of those times. He placed his hand over hers, saying, "Thanks for being honest with me." There was nothing more to say. Whatever happened with *Coaching to Win*, he now knew he had at least one person in his corner.

It was getting late. Leaving the report, he pulled at Linda's hand, and together they climbed the stairs to bed.

It was late morning the next day before Sam gave another thought to the upcoming training program. Résumés continued to trickle in for Jerry's position. As predicted, the company had widened the search to include prospects from outside. Sam had a couple of résumés on his desk that, on the surface, seemed promising. But being an old hand at this, he would reserve judgment until he'd interviewed the candidates. People who looked good on paper didn't always pan out.

Sam reached for the file folder he'd designated for his *Coaching to Win* materials. Now that he'd received the report on his behavioral assessment, he could finish the questions in the field guide and be free for the weekend. After rereading his report, he answered the questions. Satisfied he'd only spent fifteen minutes, he closed the guide and put the folder out of the way on his desk. The workweek was winding down, and thankfully there were now only two things on Sam's mind—the tasks he'd have to complete before Friday, and the weekend ahead.

Sam's weekend passed uneventfully. There always seemed to be work to do around the house—cleaning out the gutters, a minor repair to the sprinkler system. Yet with his homework done for next week's call, he felt relaxed.

The morning of the call, he was at his desk a few minutes early. At least they could do this over the phone, Sam thought. Whatever they were dishing up, it would be easy for him to listen with one ear and keep working. He still needed to analyze the production numbers, keep up with e-mail, and sift through a half dozen résumés.

The call started promptly at nine. Scott, the facilitator, invited the eight participants to introduce themselves. Sam jumped in first. Once he finished his introduction, he tuned out as he scrolled through his unread e-mails.

Following the introductions, Scott began reviewing the call agenda. Sam continued with his e-mail, feeling productive. *Who says you can't kill two birds with one stone?* he thought.

But Sam was about to get caught. He had drifted into writing a reply to an e-mail he'd received from HR. Then, as if in a dream, he heard Scott say, "You like to go first, Sam. Will you begin by sharing what the report told you about your behavioral style?"

A moment of panic brought Sam back to the conversation. He scrambled for the folder containing his report and the field guide and was able to make a smooth recovery, describing for Scott and the other participants what he'd learned about his own behavioral style.

Sam had averted embarrassment, but he'd learned his lesson. Multitasking in this environment could be hazardous to your health. He shut the window displaying his e-mail and tried to put his mind completely on the call. Once Sam gave Scott his full attention, he found that Scott was giving them some pretty helpful information.

Scott explained that the learning they were about to undertake wasn't a spectator sport. During the workshop, they would be expected to give examples in areas where they'd given themselves high scores on the coaching skills self-assessment, as well as ask questions in the areas where their self-scoring was low.

Scott stated that they'd learn the most by applying the new coaching concepts and sharing their experience with the other participants. Sam was liking the safety-in-numbers nature of that. They were all learning. They'd be able to own their mistakes as a group, as well as their successes.

He glanced at his watch. They seemed to be covering a lot of ground.

Scott went on to explain that each of them needed to select one of their direct reports to be the subject of their coaching for the next seven weeks. That selection would need to take place before the workshop.

Sensing that Scott was wrapping up, Sam's eyes traveled to a printout of the production numbers. But a second later, he thought better of it. He'd almost been caught once during the call, and he had no desire for it to happen again.

Scott explained that their direct managers would be their learning partners in this process. The assignment was to meet with these learning partners—Reggie, in Sam's case—prior to the upcoming workshop and complete two action points. The first was to agree on expectations for the training. The second was to agree on which of Sam's direct reports would be the recipient of his coaching.

Scott closed out the call, thanking them for their participation and wishing them the best. Sam hung up the phone and sat silently for a moment. He was still skeptical that any of this would happen. Reggie had barely been able to spend a half hour at breakfast with him last week. How would he find time to support Sam through the training process?

Setting that question aside, Sam got back to work—real work this time. He made some notes on the production numbers and then gave HR the green light to call in one of the candidates for an interview. Glancing through his e-mail again, Sam saw something that caused him to change the assumption he'd made only an hour ago:

☑

To:	**Reggie Dahlgren**
From:	**Scott Andrews**
cc:	**Sam Wainwright**
RE:	***Coaching to Win*—Sam Wainwright**

It was a message from Scott, the *Coaching to Win* facilitator, giving Reggie a heads-up that Sam would be contacting Reggie to schedule a meeting to discuss expectations for the training and agree on a coachee. Reggie now knew that Sam was supposed to contact him about getting together.

Refusing to let this thing snowball, Sam grabbed the phone, got Reggie on the line, and arranged a breakfast meeting for Friday. Reggie promised that he'd give it his full attention and wouldn't dash out after only half an hour. It seemed as though Reggie had to commit to this thing with both feet too. Safety in numbers, Sam thought for the second time that day. Oh well. After seven weeks, *Coaching to Win* would be a distant memory. Then he could get on with things. Important things.

The skies looked stormy as Sam pulled up to the Downtown Café. He glanced in the backseat, realizing that he'd left his umbrella at the office. He hoped the raindrops would stay away until they finished breakfast. Armed with his field guide and report, he strode in and found Reggie in the corner booth again. The men ordered coffee and their usual, and they quickly got down to business.

"First thing I want to do is share some of my *Coaching to Win* experience with you," Reggie said. Sam noted that Reggie had a copy of his own behavioral assessment report. "But before that, I want to ask you how it's going for you so far."

Sam briefly explained about the work he'd done, his report, and the conference call with Scott. "It's fine, I guess," admitted Sam, "though I still feel like I should be focusing on getting our numbers up and hiring Jerry's replacement."

Reggie smiled. "I can understand that. I had a lot going on when I was asked to take part in the training too. At first I didn't want to give it my full attention. Thought I had things that were way more important. But when I began to understand the importance of coaching and how it could affect our bottom line, I saw that nothing else was as important as this."

Sam nodded, really not sold but willing at least to give Reggie the benefit of the doubt.

"That report was a real eye-opener for me, and I hope it was for you too," Reggie went on. "Here's mine. I'd like you to take a look at it. Mind if I also take a look at yours?"

Sam hadn't expected this. It felt weird to be reading his boss's report, but fair was fair, as Reggie was about to read his. They exchanged sheaves of papers. The waitress poured more coffee, and the two men sat in silence for a time, digesting the contents of each others' findings.

Reggie spoke first. "Interesting," he remarked. "I see a couple of areas where we're both very much alike." Sam smiled at the apparent good news. "We're both pretty social guys," Reggie went on, "and we also share a dislike for getting bogged down in details. We can help each other there, so things don't fall through the cracks."

This was not what Sam had expected. Reggie didn't seem upset about any of this. Sam liked the direction this discussion was going, and he began to relax.

Reggie continued, "I'll bet the first time you read this, your reaction was typical of most people. They skip over the positive parts and focus on areas they don't feel are positive. I know I did. But a big part of this training is also getting you to recognize your strengths."

To emphasize his point, Reggie turned to page 5 of the report, reeling off a litany of Sam's strengths—his ability to always invent something new, his willingness to take positive risks and accept change.

"Here's something else that's helpful," Reggie said. "Our reports indicate that our communication styles are very similar. So it will be easy for us to stay on the same wavelength."

The more Reggie talked, the more Sam was encouraged. Reggie emphasized the importance of figuring out ways for them to put this information to work in the warehouse. The discussion grew animated, and they hardly realized that forty-five minutes had passed. Sam wasn't 100 percent clear yet on how this would all help get the numbers up, but it felt like a step in the right direction.

What were clear, however, were Reggie's expectations of him. "We need to discuss who you're going to choose as your coachee for the training period. That will be the only person you'll be coaching over the next seven weeks. After that, I expect you to use what you've learned to coach all of your direct reports."

Sam tried to mask his frustration. He could barely imagine the time it was going to take to apply this training to one of his direct reports. Now Reggie wanted it for all of them. Not forgetting the need to get the numbers back up and to solve a major staffing issue.

Reading Sam's look, Reggie was reassuring. "Look, I know what you're thinking. But it's doable, trust me." Moving on, Reggie asked, "Have you given any thought to whom you'd like to choose as your coachee?"

"I was thinking about Nick," Sam answered, describing his feeling that Nick had the talent to move up with the right coaching.

"Excellent!" Reggie said.

Sam could feel his boss's support. Having Reggie on his side was a big plus, and Sam was beginning to see the possibility for a new kind of relationship that would benefit both of them. He only hoped his direct reports might over time come to feel the same way about him.

"One last thing," said Reggie. "You know you have a full day of training coming up Wednesday, right?"

Sam nodded.

Reggie asked, "Just curious—what's your plan for keeping the home fires burning while you're doing the training?"

It was a good question, and Sam really hadn't given it much thought. But wanting to demonstrate to Reggie that he could think on his feet, he offered, "I figured that I'd do the training, but check in with my guys during the breaks and over lunch."

Reggie smiled. He knew how hard this was going to be for Sam, and he was sympathetic. "Don't make my mistake," he told Sam. "At first, I wasn't willing to give all this the time of day either. Thought I could multitask it with the rest of my workload. Even tried doing my expense reports during the initial conference call."

Sam smiled, remembering how he'd also tried to multitask during his own call.

"Trust your guys," Reggie suggested. "They can manage the place for one day."

Sam looked at Reggie. He wanted to believe it, that the warehouse wouldn't come crashing down if he was gone for a day. As long as Reggie was supporting him, he'd have to give it a try.

Sam recalled something he'd heard a long time ago, an axiom of sorts. If you want someone to be trustworthy, first you have to trust him. Maybe it was time to stop carrying the entire warehouse on his shoulders.

It was still overcast as Sam left the restaurant, but luckily the rain had stayed away. Driving back to work, he thought about checking the field guide and seeing what he needed to do to prepare for the all-day session. He'd stick to the seminar Wednesday. His guys could handle things. Besides, he told himself, he could use a day's vacation.

Your Turn to Win: Take the Coaching Skills Self-Assessment That Sam and Reggie Took

Coaching Skills Self-Assessment
Rating Scale

1 = Never 2 = Rarely 3 = Sometimes 4 = Usually 5 = Always
Coaching Skills Rating

1. I communicate in a clear and effective way. _____

2. I actively look for ways to engage and motivate my direct reports. _____

3. When discussing development, I focus on both strengths and improvement areas. _____

4. I focus on developing strengths that will result in achieving critical business goals. _____

5. I create an environment that encourages effective communication and exchange of ideas. _____

6. I focus my full attention on my coachee during our discussions. _____

7. I paraphrase what my coachee says to ensure that we understand each other. _____

8. I listen to what my coachee has to say before I respond. _____

9. I ask questions to engage my coachee in dialogue. _____

10. I give feedback so that my coachee understands how his/her efforts help the company meet business goals. _____

11. I encourage my coachee to develop his/her own solutions to problems. _____

12. I summarize discussions by stating the next steps we agreed upon. _____

13. I provide my coachee with information and resources to meet his/her professional goals. _____

14. I assure my coachee of my commitment to his/her success. _____

15. I encourage my coachee to evaluate his/her progress toward reaching his/her goals. _____

16. I update goals and next steps when changes occur. _____

17. I congratulate my coachee on his/her successes and help him/her overcome barriers. _____

18. I recognize my coachee for a job well done. _____

19. I challenge and encourage my coachee to continuously improve. _____

20. I recognize the importance of creating a positive work environment. _____

ment, answer the following
questions:*

1. List the three statements where you rated yourself the highest:

How can you leverage these skills even further to increase your
effectiveness as a leader and coach?

2. List the three statements where you rated yourself the lowest:

What specific activities will help you develop in these areas?

Choose and record one thing you will commit to doing differently from
this moment forward to leverage your strengths in new ways and/or
close gaps to make yourself a more effective leader and coach.

Chapter Four

BASIC TRAINING

Wednesday, 7:42 a.m.

It was hard for Sam to separate all the emotions he was feeling as he set out that morning for his all-day *Coaching to Win* workshop. He felt a strange mixture of nerves and excitement, a sensation that took him back to when he'd decided to go after his degree in supply chain management. It wasn't a bad feeling, more like a sense of expectation. His gut told him that this would all be good for him in the long run. The sky was a brilliant blue as he got out of the car with his field guide in hand and headed in.

A sign in the lobby directed him to the training room down the hall. As Sam walked in, he observed about two dozen participants milling around, getting coffee and doughnuts from a table against the far wall. He was hoping to see somebody he knew. Instead, he saw only unfamiliar faces.

Sam hesitated. Many of the other men were smartly attired in khaki slacks and brightly colored polo shirts: the corporate guys. Sam had always felt a little uncomfortable around those guys, who never seemed to get their hands dirty. He thought of his own clothes. The standard warehouse uniform consisted of sturdy work pants and a button-up shirt worn over a T-shirt, and scuffed up, steel-toed shoes. He shrugged. His uniform had been good enough for him for twenty-five years, and it would do for today. They were here to learn, not trade fashion tips.

As Sam advanced into the room, a large, athletically built man broke from a conversation and approached him. Thrusting out his meaty hand, he said, "Hi, Sam. I'm Scott, the facilitator for today. Welcome to phase 2 of *Coaching to Win*." Sam recognized Scott's voice from the conference call. "Grab some coffee," Scott suggested, glancing up at the clock. "We'll get started right at eight. You're welcome to sit anywhere—just write your name on the table tent at your seat."

Sam grabbed a cup of coffee, bypassed the doughnuts, and headed for one of the round tables already populated by four other participants. General greetings were exchanged. Sam took a seat and wrote his name on the table tent with bold, even strokes.

The table was now full. Feeling nervous, he flipped through the blue-and-green workshop binder in front of him. The men on either side of him soon introduced themselves, which made Sam feel more at ease. He regretted judging them on their attire; they were actually nice guys. Maybe it was going to be okay.

Promptly at eight, Scott took his position in the front of the room, and the session began. Sam looked up at the clock, wondering how he'd stay focused until five that afternoon. His thoughts drifted back to the warehouse. He wondered how many things would come up today that needed his attention. It would be a good test, he decided. His guys could handle things for a day. Sam's mind came back into the room.

Scott posed an interesting question. "Think about somebody," he said, "who made a significant impact on your life." He directed participants to page 2 of the field guide's workshop section, asking them to record their answers.

Sam looked around the room, watching the others reflecting on Scott's question. Some were smiling. All were thoughtful.

Allowing them several minutes to think and write, Scott waited for their heads to come up. Then he asked, "Is anybody willing to share with us who their significant person was?"

To Sam's surprise, a number of hands went up immediately. Scott called on a man near the coffee table, who described a former supervisor who had strongly impacted his life.

Sam's hand stayed down. He still felt a little nervous, not quite ready to share. He glanced down at the page in his guide where he had written the name Don Stovall.

Mr. Stovall had been Sam's high school baseball coach. Always stocky and not the fastest runner on the team, Sam was nevertheless a powerful guy with a bat. Coach Stovall realized that Sam's true talent was as a hitter, and he'd worked with him to hone that skill to a fine edge. He never seemed worried that Sam didn't get any faster around the bases—they had other guys on the team who could run like the wind. Coach Stovall could see the unique strengths of each of his players. He had a gift for helping them develop those strengths.

Sam left his reverie as the program moved on. Scott spoke about the relationship between leadership skills and performance. "There is a direct correlation between your effectiveness as leaders and what kind of performance you get from the people who report to you." He went on to describe three categories of performance and how they related to leadership styles. Poor leaders get unacceptable performance. Coercive leaders get "acceptable" performance—people performing at a level just good enough to keep their jobs. Only effective leaders elicit outstanding performance from their direct reports, in an environment where they "want to" excel rather than feeling like they "have to" in order not to be fired.

All this caused Sam to reflect on his own leadership skills. He thought of the lagging production numbers. In Sam's analysis, his guys just weren't trying hard enough. So what was Scott saying here? Was it Sam's fault? Did the real reason for the poor numbers have more to do with a deficiency in his leadership skills than the commitment of his workers?

It seemed like a key question, one that Sam would have liked to noodle on further. But Scott was moving on, and Sam wanted to stay with him.

Next, Scott introduced something he called the PEnS Coaching Model, saying that great coaching doesn't happen by accident. Rather, effective coaches use models to guide them. There were three parts to the PEnS acronym: preparing, engaging, and sustaining. Sam liked this. Anything that would make this stuff easy to remember.

Scott continued by discussing the preparing piece of this coaching model, which had to do with them preparing for their first session with their coachees. He also said they'd be practicing throughout the day.

Sam's stomach took a turn at the word *practicing*. *Thanks, Reggie,* he thought. Reggie hadn't said one word about role-playing being part of this workshop. And to be sure, there were few things in life that Sam disliked more. Still, he didn't have time to stew, as Scott was moving on.

Scott broke down the first step of the PEnS Coaching Model. Preparing to work with a coachee involved three key elements:

1) Defining your coaching objective
2) Assessing yourself, your coachee, and the relationship between the two of you
3) Planning the dialogue

Next, Scott asked them to pull out something called the *Coaching to Win* action plan. This was the worksheet on which participants were asked to write down the coaching objective for their coachee.

Sam recalled how he and Reggie had agreed to coach Nick on streamlining the warehouse's order fulfillment process. His hunch was that somewhere in that process, there were bottlenecks and inefficiencies. These culprits probably kept the warehouse from hitting its numbers. Sam neatly printed *Streamline the order fulfillment process* in the space provided on the action plan and looked up, waiting for the next instruction.

As the group finished writing their objectives, Scott directed them to lay the action plan aside while he described the next step in the preparation process: the assessment. "The first step is to assess yourself," Scott said.

He took some time to discuss behavioral styles and the importance of being able to adjust when your style differs from your coachee. The discussion made Sam reflect on the conversation he and Reggie had had a few days earlier. Sam's and Reggie's behavioral styles were quite similar; little adjustment would be needed there. Sam did wonder, however, what Nick's style would be, and how it might require him to adjust his own style to be an effective coach.

What followed was a learning section that required a lot of interaction. The point was to be able to identify different behavioral styles and "flex" or adjust your own style to complement that of your coachee, making the coaching relationship more successful.

Sam found he was getting into the workshop more than he'd thought he would. A lot of things were beginning to click with him, like why he'd found Jerry so easy to talk to, while communicating with some of the others was so challenging. It all had to do with this concept of behavioral styles. Sam now saw how flexing his own style could make things a lot easier. *One new trick for the old dog,* he thought with a smile.

And there was more relief in store. As the group reviewed their coaching skills self-assessments, Sam learned that he was not alone. Nobody in the class was perfect. All of them had things to learn, things they could improve on.

Now Scott shifted their focus to assessing their coachees. The process was familiar—he would send a link to Nick for the behavioral assessment. Sam's first meeting with Nick would be to share, compare, and understand each other's behavioral styles, exactly as Sam and Reggie had done. Pieces were beginning to fall into place, and Sam's confidence was growing. In spite of what had to get done back at the warehouse, this was a ball he could probably juggle along with everything else.

Scott told the group that there was one more thing he'd like to cover before the lunch break. It had to do with assessing the current relationships they had with their intended coachees.

Sam thought about Nick. His relationship with Nick certainly wasn't as strong as the one he had with Jerry. On the positive side, however, he and Nick had no big issues either. Sam listened as other participants asked questions. From the nature of those questions, it was clear that these guys had some repair work ahead of them with their coachees—obstacles that would need to be overcome for the coaching to work. Again, Sam felt relieved. His relationship with Nick was a blank canvas, ready to be painted.

They took a brief lunch break, grabbing sandwiches from the table. The group was coming together. Animated conversations went on all around the room. The spirit was upbeat. They were all in this together, and it felt like a team, everyone working toward a common goal.

After lunch, Sam was energized. As each hour passed, the group grew more comfortable. He even could recall a handful of other guys' first names, in addition to the ones sitting at his own table.

When everyone was seated, Scott began again, this time describing the process for planning the dialogue with their coachees. He broke the planning concept down into what he called the Three *P*s: purpose, process, and payoff.

Purpose was simply the reason for your discussion. Process was defining how you and your coachee would interact, and Sam was already thinking how he might flex his style when interacting with Nick. The third *P*, payoff, was identifying how the coaching would benefit you, your coachee, and the company.

Scott had a way of breaking things down into bite-size chunks that Sam really liked. He had a feeling that this stuff would stay in his head until he could use it with Nick, and ultimately with all his direct reports.

Now Scott posed another question. "How many times have you walked away from a discussion," he asked, "and thought, 'Well, that didn't go like I thought it would'?"

A collective chuckle went around the room. Scott smiled at the reaction and continued, "There's a reason for that. Often, it's because if we plan a discussion at all, we focus only on the words we want to say."

Sam thought back to the initial meeting he'd had with his warehouse supervisors after Jerry had given his notice. Scott was right. Sam had thought only of what he wanted to tell them. And he remembered how that had turned out.

"What you want to tell them is only one part of the communication process," Scott went on. "Here's another tool that will help you. It's called Know/Do/Feel. Number one: What do you want your coachee to *know*? Number two: What do you want your coachee to *do*? And finally, number three: What do you want your coachee to *feel*?"

When people plan at all, Scott told them, they spend time thinking about the *know* and *do* pieces, but generally skip the *feel* piece altogether. The discipline of Know/Do/Feel requires you to think not only about the message, but also about how that message will be received by your coachee.

Scott described the advantage in this: "If you cover all three pieces, it helps you craft a specific, targeted message and have a stronger handle on the discussion, because you've decided in advance how you want your coachee to feel.

"Learn to watch for the indicators," Scott suggested. "If you want the person you're coaching to feel encouraged and supported, then look for the signs that they're feeling that. On the other hand, if you sense that they're getting defensive or showing some other emotion, you can adjust in the moment and bring them back. Much better than leaving the discussion thinking it didn't go like you planned, right?"

Heads nodded around the room. Again, Sam thought of the meeting he'd had with his supervisors where he hadn't invited Jerry. He'd given no thought to the *feel* piece in that discussion, the thing that could have completely changed the outcome. Still, he wasn't down on himself. Nobody had a perfect track record. That was why they were here. And whatever had happened in the past, Sam was determined not to make the same mistakes again.

Scott directed them back to their action plans. Now that everyone had a better understanding of the Three *P*s and Know/Do/Feel, they could finish their preparation notes. Sam finished his quickly, looking around the room as the other guys continued to write. He felt good, like he was picking up speed. He sat back in his chair and waited for the others to finish.

As their attention returned to the front, Scott said, "Now choose a partner. We're going to do a little practice."

A wave of indigestion hit Sam's stomach. Practice. It was the moment he'd been dreading since he first came through the training room door. Scott seemed like a smart guy. Couldn't he figure out a way to do this workshop without role-playing? Did anybody like role-playing?

He shot a nervous look at Chris, the IT guy sitting to his right. As their eyes met, Sam knew that Chris was in the same boat, hoping he could spontaneously disappear and skip this part of the *Coaching to Win* experience. The saying "Misery loves company" had never been truer than now. Sam and Chris agreed to grit their teeth and just do it, trying not to make it too awful for either one of them.

Sam decided to get it over with and go first. He shared his objective with Chris: streamline the order fulfillment process.

Chris looked at Sam for a moment and then replied, "Okay, Sam. I'm an IT guy and don't really know the warehouse. So this may sound like a dumb question, but what are you really trying to accomplish with streamlining the process? Are you trying to go faster? Save money? Reduce your head count?"

Chris was right, Sam thought. He had an objective, but it needed a finer point. Grabbing his action plan and a pencil, he added the following: streamline the order fulfillment process, increase fulfillment to 95 percent or higher, and increase accuracy while decreasing operating costs.

Sam sat back and read it several times. It sounded like a lot to handle, and he wondered if he was being fair to Nick. This was no small task. He considered rewriting it a third time, but recalled something Scott had said earlier in the workshop, that people will live up to your expectations. Not a bad thing to set the bar high. He'd see if Nick was up to a challenge. And if he succeeded, it would be big wins all the way around—for Nick, for Sam and his newly minted coaching skills, and for the company.

Sam checked the clock. The afternoon was flying by. After they finished the preparing step, the group discussed how to successfully engage their coachees. Scott had a handy acronym to help them remember this too:

C	Create a setting for coaching
O	Open-ended questions
A	Active listening
C	Collaborate and confirm
H	Help and encourage

As Scott took them through each piece of the COACH model, Sam felt more and more confident. His apprehension about the workshop was melting away. Instead of dishing out lofty theories that would be hard to understand, let alone apply, Scott was giving them practical tools that could be easily implemented. This wasn't rocket science after all.

He could already see how this stuff would be effective back in the warehouse. It wouldn't even require a radical change from what he was doing now—just paying attention and reading people a little better and then flexing his own style to complement theirs. Sam could see that it wouldn't suck up a lot of his time, either. In fact, he was optimistic that as he became more proficient in these coaching techniques, they would actually save time.

The rest of the day was devoted to work on their action plans and practicing with each other. No longer sheepish about role-playing, Sam and Chris created a real synergy between themselves. They had to admit that they were actually having fun, something they couldn't have imagined only a few hours ago.

No longer holding back, Sam found his hand going up first when Scott asked them to share with the group. With each interaction, he got new ideas that helped him fine-tune his approach. He saw the benefit in getting the bugs worked out of his plan before he even sat down for his first coaching with Nick.

Scott now focused on the last step of the PEnS model, the piece called sustaining. "This is all about how you're going to observe and evaluate your coachee's progress," Scott said. "Based on what you see, you will need to reinforce their efforts if they stay on course, or redirect those efforts if they stray from the course."

Sam redoubled his concentration. He knew that he had a lot to learn about giving effective feedback. During this segment, Scott detailed how to deliver feedback that was helpful whether the coachee was on or off track. He shared another tool that was useful in discovering why a coachee was off track.

Sam now saw why Reggie was so high on the *Coaching to Win* method. Rather than make things more complicated, the workshop was taking the mystery out of leadership. He experienced another emotion he hadn't anticipated: an eagerness to return to the warehouse and start using the skills he had learned.

The workshop was nearing its end. In closing, Scott addressed the group. "Now your real learning begins," he told them. Sam's eyebrows went up. Hadn't they already learned a ton today? Scott clarified,

"Unless you go out there and start doing this stuff immediately, it will fade. It's 'Use it or lose it.'"

He went on to explain that they would now be moving into phase 3 of the *Coaching to Win* program. "Phase 3 is designed to keep today's lessons sharp in your minds." Scott told them they'd receive a weekly e-mail for the next five weeks, outlining a fifteen-minute reading assignment. They were also expected to work with their coachees and participate in a conference call with the facilitator and the other coaches. The call would give them an opportunity to check in with each other, share their progress, and give and receive help where needed.

Scott asked if there were any final questions. No hands shot up this time. He thanked them for their attention and wished them the best in the next phase of the program.

As Sam readied to leave, he was surprised to see that nobody was dashing out. In fact, there seemed to be a collective desire to prolong the connection they'd made during the course of the day. They talked in small groups, exchanged phone numbers and e-mail addresses, and promised to stay in touch.

The traffic was crawling along as Sam headed home. For once, however, he didn't mind. He'd checked his phone before he set out, surprised that there were no voice mails from work. Even more surprising was the fact that he hadn't worried about things back at the warehouse at all. He'd kept his promise to Reggie and allowed himself to stay with the workshop. Magically, everything else had taken care of itself.

The high Sam felt from his *Coaching to Win* experience lingered, and he felt like celebrating. He gave his wife a quick buzz to let her know dinner was on him tonight, and then he detoured to Marino's Pizza. Something special had happened today, and he could lay off the calorie and cholesterol counting for one night. Inside Marino's, he breathed the intoxicating smells of garlic and Romano cheese. Suddenly, he was ravenously hungry. All that learning had given him quite an appetite. He paid for the pizza and made his way home.

As they ate, Sam shared his day with Linda: his initial fears going into the workshop, the role-playing, and how it had all turned around. Linda listened as Sam talked excitedly about his day.

Finally, there was one piece of pizza left in the box. They decided to split it. "You haven't said much," Sam told her between bites.

Linda laughed. "I didn't want to interrupt your flow," she replied. "It's just good to see you so happy. I haven't seen you so excited about anything work-related for a long time."

Sam knew she was right. He also knew that his work was cut out for him. He still had to get through phase 3. But tonight was about basking in the moment.

Together, they walked out onto the deck. Towel in hand, Linda wiped the heavy dew from the deck chairs. Enjoying the stillness of the twilight, they sat and gazed up as stars began to appear in the evening sky. Things would be just fine, Sam thought. He now had the tools to win. He was ready to practice.

Your Turn to Win: You may have missed the actual workshop, but here's your chance to participate as Sam did and gain tools and insight in the art of coaching.

1. *Name one person who has had a significant impact on your life, someone whose belief in you inspired you to do more than you thought was possible:*

2. *Describe your relationship with that person, and why it was significant:*

3. *What specifically did that person say or do that drew the best out of you?*

4. *How can you use what you discovered above to inspire the same level of performance from those whom you influence?*

5. *Choose and record one thing you will commit to doing differently from this moment forward to be the type of leader who brings out the best in others:*

Chapter Five

DIVING IN

Thursday, 9:02 a.m.

Sam felt different today. Part of it was being away from the warehouse yesterday for the *Coaching to Win* workshop. Days off were rare for him, especially in the last year. The odd feeling, however, wasn't at all bad. Sam now felt like he had an agenda, a way of getting at solutions rather than wading through the same old problems. He could feel the energy from the workshop follow him into work.

First order of business was to check in with his crew and catch up on what had happened the previous day. He'd shot his guys a quick e-mail, and by nine the three warehouse supervisors were in Sam's office. There wasn't much to tell, but their body language spoke volumes. They were leaning into the discussion instead of leaning back like the last time. No one crossed his arms. And there was a different energy. It was subtle, but it was there. He sensed that they were beginning to show more enthusiasm, take a little more ownership of things.

Satisfied, Sam moved on to their plan for covering Jerry's role until a replacement was hired. Nick acted as spokesman for the group, laying out what they were recommending. No surprises there either. It was pretty much what Sam would have implemented himself without their input. However, they had added a nuance or two that told him they'd really thought it through. "That all sounds good," he heard himself saying, and he encouraged them to get things rolling.

Craig, who seemed the most direct of the warehouse supervisors, addressed Sam. "Will we get any say in who takes Jerry's place?" Sam thought for a moment. The question had caught him off guard. "After all," Craig went on, "whoever you hire will affect all of us."

Sam knew Craig was right. His guys had shown that they could make useful contributions, so he tested the waters. "What were you thinking about?" he asked.

"Well, I don't know," Craig replied. "Maybe help look through the applications for Jerry's spot, help you with initial interviews, stuff like that."

It made sense. If Sam could empower these guys to help with the search, it might speed up the process and give him more time to coach Nick. He thought back to that deal about people supporting the things they help create. This could also be a way of ensuring that they'd support Jerry's replacement when he came on board. "Sounds like a good idea," Sam told them. "Be sure you coordinate with HR so we do things according to company policy. I will make the final decision, but you can help us get to a short list. Give me your top picks."

Sam read the room. It was clear that he had made the right call to enlist their help. The guys seemed genuinely enthusiastic, glad to have a meaningful part in the hiring process. He thanked them for handling things the previous day, and the meeting broke up.

Nick was last out of the door, but stopped when Sam said, "Hey, Nick, got a minute?" Nick stopped, turned around, and approached Sam's desk.

"Have a seat," Sam invited. "I just need a minute." When Nick was seated, Sam made his pitch. He described the *Coaching to Win* program he was going through. "That's why I was gone yesterday," Sam added. "We had an all-day workshop, one of the best I've ever been to."

Now he'd reached the moment of truth. Explaining that the program took place over eight weeks, Sam told Nick that part of his requirement was to coach one of his direct reports during that time frame. "I'd like you to be that person," he said, his throat feeling a little dry. "What do you think?"

Nick eyed him, and Sam felt uncomfortable. What if Nick said, "No, thanks"? Until this moment, he'd taken for granted that Nick would agree. If the man didn't, Sam felt like he'd be back to the drawing board.

He'd have to basically rethink the whole thing. He also knew Nick was the best choice for this process improvement assignment.

Sam's fears, however, proved to be unfounded. A moment later, Nick broke into a big grin and said, "Sure thing." Relieved, Sam thanked him and the two shook hands. Nick was now officially his coachee. They were off and running.

Briefly, Sam told Nick about the behavioral assessment that would start the process. "I'll send you the link," Sam said. "I think you'll find it interesting." He also let Nick know he'd be e-mailing him a meeting invitation to discuss the findings of his assessment and talk about their objective for the coaching. Sam noted Nick's body language: open posture, sitting forward in the chair. Both good signs.

The discussion ended, and Nick rose to go, but Sam stopped him in the doorway. "Hey, just something to keep in mind," he told his coachee. "This is the first time on this for me. There may be some bumps. I'm learning too."

Nick merely smiled. "No problem, boss," he said, and they both got back to work.

Sam was pleased. The whole thing had gone much better than he expected. He shot Nick the link to the behavioral assessment, then an invitation for their follow-up meeting on Monday afternoon. Something told him that Nick would get right on the assessment, and he was right. Before the end of the day, he'd received Nick's e-mail informing him that the assessment was complete and Nick had already received his report on the findings. Sam sent an encouraging reply and said that he was looking forward to their meeting Monday.

Friday brought a new set of production numbers, no worse than the last, but certainly no better. It increased Sam's fever to get this process improvement going as soon as possible. He experienced a moment of doubt, wondering if Nick would really be able to step up to the plate. It was also Sam's first go at this new coaching process. The pressure would be on both of them. Still, he chose to be optimistic. As he reminded himself, he'd have Scott and those other guys on their weekly call for support and to keep him on track.

Sam treated Linda to a date night Saturday—dinner at their favorite steak house and a movie. He found it a little easier to relax on weekends now, and over T-bones and twice-baked potatoes, he shared with her the good news that Nick had accepted his coaching offer.

"You and Nick are really different personalities," Linda noted. "I remember when you introduced him to me. He was really very quiet. How do you think that's going to work out?"

Sam shared with her what he'd learned from the workshop about flexing his style to complement differing personality types. Listening to himself, he was proud that the lessons from the workshop were beginning to take hold. *If I can explain it to someone,* he thought, *that means I can probably do it.*

Monday came, and before the afternoon meeting with Nick, Sam reviewed his action plan so it would be fresh in his mind. As he read through it, he felt confident. He was glad that this program allowed him ample time to practice and refine his coaching skills. Pulling out the field guide, he finished the reading assignment for this week's call. It would be hard to do anything more until he got some insight into Nick's behavioral style.

Sam had brown-bagged it, a turkey sandwich on wheat and an apple, which he consumed at his desk. While he was eating, Craig stuck his head in. The warehouse supervisors had culled the applicants for Jerry's job down to four they felt deserved interviews. The two discussed next steps, and Craig left to follow up with HR. When he was gone, Sam realized that the whole weekend had gone by and he hadn't worried about Jerry's replacement once. It might have been a small victory, but Sam gave himself a silent three cheers anyway. He was learning to let go.

Nick was prompt. He showed himself at Sam's door right at two o'clock. The symmetry of the meeting wasn't lost on Sam. He'd sat across from Reggie in a similar fashion not long ago as their coaching relationship began. First, he thanked Nick for being a willing guinea pig. Sam also laid out the schedule, telling him that for the next five weeks, they'd be meeting weekly to discuss the project that Nick would be charged with.

He noticed that Nick's eyes kept shifting to the folder in his lap that Sam assumed contained Nick's behavioral assessment report. "So, how did you like doing the assessment?" Sam inquired, hoping to break the ice. He could feel Nick's guard was up, so he waited patiently for a response.

After a moment, Nick said, "Well, I guess it was okay. I mean, there was some stuff that was a little hard to swallow, but mostly it was right on, pretty accurate about my behavior."

"That's about what I felt when I got my report," Sam reassured him. "I even showed it to my wife, hoping she'd back me up, disagree with the things I disagreed with. Instead, she told me it was spot-on!"

"Ouch," said Nick, and they shared a chuckle. The tension was now broken. Sam offered his report to Nick and asked if Nick would share his. Papers were exchanged, and the men read in silence.

Sam spoke first. "It's interesting," he told Nick. "Mine says I like to try new things, and yours says you also like to look into new things. That's important here, because I believe this project we're about to discuss will get the creative juices flowing for both of us."

Sam also noted where there were distinct differences in their behavioral styles. Details were Nick's comfort zone; Sam really didn't care about getting bogged down in the details of anything. They agreed for this coaching exercise, Nick wouldn't overwhelm Sam with too many details. Rather, he would bottom-line things for Sam in his reporting. Sam explained this adjustment as "flexing your behavioral style." Nick nodded and jotted notes on his pad.

"There's one other difference in our behavior," Sam went on. "I know I'm the kind of guy who loves to shoot the breeze, but you're not." Sam was now putting another piece into place, recalling how Nick would make himself scarce whenever he and Jerry launched into one of their "Who's better: Chicago Bears or St. Louis Rams?" conversations. Sam promised to spare Nick from that in the future, and Nick's smile told him he appreciated the football reprieve.

The meeting was going smoothly, which Sam again credited to his preparation. The next step was to share the coaching objective he'd come up with. Putting his action plan on the desk between them, he watched as Nick read the objective: Streamline the order fulfillment process to increase fulfillment to 95 percent or higher while increasing accuracy and decreasing operating costs.

Nick let out a deep breath and sat back in his chair. He looked at Sam with a combination of fear and enthusiasm. Sam said, "Look, I know it's challenging. But I also think you're up to it. Your assessment shows me that you're the right man for the job. You're able to look at things from different angles, which is critical in this case. I mean, we can't keep doing exactly what we've been doing and expect to get our numbers up, right?" Nick nodded in agreement.

"Here's the other thing," Sam continued. "Your report indicates that you have a knack for making things systematic. That's another huge plus for us in this project." He gave Nick a moment, knowing that there was a lot to consider. Then he said, "You know, we're not after the perfect solution here. What we're out to achieve is a significant process improvement. If we can get that, we'll have succeeded."

Sam explained that they'd be meeting weekly for the next five weeks to talk about progress and identify any barriers. "I want you to take the lead on this, but I'm behind you 100 percent." He realized that he'd been doing most of the talking while Nick had remained mostly silent. It was now Sam's turn to sit back. "Well, what do you think?" he asked.

Nick's expression, which had been thoughtful throughout, suddenly broke into a broad smile. "Let's go for it!" he said with enthusiasm. "Go Bears! Go Rams!"

Sam had to laugh out loud. Nick was the right man for the job. And he now knew that Nick also had a real sense of humor.

If there had been a football in reach, Sam would have spiked it. He may not have won the game yet, but the operative word was *yet*. And he'd made an important first down. Nick was willing to go for it; the rest would come. Sam decided a pat on the back was in order. All the preparation had paid off. *Imagine that*, he thought. Before the workshop, he would have just winged the meeting. And now he could see a dramatic difference in the result.

On Wednesday after lunch—ham, low-fat swiss, and light mayo on rye—Sam returned to his field guide, answering questions in preparation for Thursday's conference call. Lunch at his desk was getting to be a habit—a good habit. Foregoing the fast-food forays that had been his norm, he had actually dropped four pounds in the past two weeks. Twenty-minute walks in the evening with Linda were also helping, taking away from his waistline and giving him back more quality time with his wife. This coaching stuff seemed to be giving him momentum outside the office. Things he'd put off for too long were now much easier to get his teeth into.

He reflected again about all the differences between his behavioral style and Nick's. Sam would definitely have to make some changes. Momentarily, he thought how much easier this process would have been if Jerry were his coachee. On the plus side, however, he figured Nick would give him plenty of practice in flexing his style. And if Sam could make the adjustments successfully with Nick, he could coach anybody.

The last question in the field guide asked Sam to reflect on the dialogue with his coachee that week, and describe both the things that were successful and those that could be improved in the future. He thought about his interactions with Nick since their meeting. These conversations now seemed easier than before. Was it his imagination? He felt a new openness coming from Nick. He noticed himself talking less and listening more. He made a mental note to ask Linda if his listening skills were improving. She, if anyone, would tell him the truth.

Thursday morning came, and Sam was ready. No multitasking this time. He had cleared the desk so he could give his full attention to Scott and the other participants on the call. Closing his office door, he took a sip of hot coffee, used the dial-in number, and then punched the access code. At the top of the hour, Scott went through introductions and moved immediately into the discussion.

Asking if they had their field guides in front of them, Scott invited participants to share their responses to the questions about their initial coaching sessions. Surprisingly, Sam heard himself speak up first. He told the group about his preparation for the session with his coachee and relayed his coachee's enthusiasm to take on the project. "I tried to keep it low-key," Sam said, explaining the differences between his and his coachee's behavioral styles. "I guess I played it right," Sam concluded, "and it looks like we're off to a good start."

Another participant, Lana, was next to weigh in. She described a first coaching session that hadn't come off as well. Scott took Lana through a series of questions, trying to get at what had happened. It appeared that Lana hadn't prepared adequately before meeting with her coachee. "Maybe I should have thought it through more beforehand," admitted Lana. "But I work in accounting, and we've got all these audits going. My big problem right now is no time."

Again Sam spoke up. He could hear the frustration in Lana's voice, so his tone was gentle. "That used to be my easy out too. I had this idea that I was too busy, that I had enough on my plate already and couldn't work on anything else." He went on to reinforce that the prep really didn't take much time. "In fact, it probably saved me time, because now we're moving forward, and I don't have to have the same meeting over again to try and fix things." To illustrate, Sam shared his experience of the two meetings he'd conducted with his warehouse supervisors about covering Jerry's job. "If I'd really thought it through, that second meeting wouldn't have had to happen."

The call wrapped up with Scott reminding everyone to complete next week's assignment. He also encouraged them to reach out to him directly in the interim if they had questions. Good-byes were heard all around, and Sam softly hung up the phone. Luck was still with him. He felt good about the whole thing—his success with Nick, not being afraid to jump right into the discussion, and sharing his story with Lana. This thing seemed to be in full gear now, and he was eager to see what process improvement Nick would come up with for their next meeting.

Sam's satisfaction carried him to the end of the day. The hunt for Jerry's replacement was moving ahead, mostly through the efforts of his guys. A few weeks earlier, he would have shouldered the whole thing himself. As he drove home, he saw something else. For years, he'd had a tendency to sweat the traffic, irritated by slow-downs, sometimes using colorful language if someone cut him off or followed too close. But that day, he actually sat back in his seat and simply enjoyed the ride.

That night he sat with his beer and heard about Linda's day. Relaxing after work was getting easier, too—and Sam knew it wasn't just the Heineken.

Jane Pierce

Linda held out a paint swatch for the kitchen walls. "It's called 'Oasis Green,'" she said brightly. "What do you think?"

Sam took the swatch, squinted, and held it up to the wall. "I think it's beautiful," he said. Dinner would be ready soon.

They sat quietly for a moment. At last, Linda spoke. "Thanks for listening," she said.

"You're welcome," Sam replied. *Listening.* Then he thought, *And I didn't even need to ask.*

Your Turn to Win: Eventually, you will want to coach each of your direct reports. For now, focus on one person and one goal or coaching objective.

1. Selection Criteria—Using the criteria below, select one of your direct reports with whom to begin refining your coaching skills. Choose someone who

   a) is working on an important/challenging goal from his/her goal plan;
   b) is willing to be coached;
   c) is meeting your expectations in his/her overall performance;
   d) has experience in his/her current job; and
   e) is free of difficult, pressing, and immediate coaching challenges.

Who will be your coachee for this learning experience?

2. Coaching Objective—Now that you've decided whom to coach, the next step is to decide on your coaching objective.

Setting the Goal—What is one important goal or challenge your coachee is working on? Or, if you have recently given them an important assignment, like Sam had for Nick, what is that assignment?

Measuring Success—How will you measure the success of the assignment? In other words, what specifically are you looking to accomplish? Think about the assignment Sam gave Nick. It wasn't only to streamline the order fulfillment process, as Sam initially thought. It was to streamline the order fulfillment process, increase fulfillment to 95 percent or higher, and increase accuracy while decreasing operating costs. State your coaching objective here, complete with how you will measure its success.

3. Relationship Check—Before starting, consider the existing relationship between you and your coachee. If your relationship is long and strong, that's *great*! You're ahead of the game. If, however, you've had a strained relationship with this coachee in the past, take time up front to share what you're doing and why you selected him or her. Be candid that you are learning new coaching techniques and appreciate the coachee's willingness to be coached. Say that you want to start by healing any injuries to your relationship that occurred in the past. When you share with your coachee that you selected him or her because of the importance of the chosen goal, you begin validating that what the coachee is doing is important to him/her, to you, and to the company.

Assess the Relationship with your coachee. Is there any groundwork you need to do before you begin this coaching adventure? If so, what specifically is your plan?

Chapter Six

IRONING THINGS OUT

Friday, 10:30 a.m.

The work week was rapidly ending. It was Friday morning, and Sam's warehouse supervisors had asked to meet with him about Jerry's replacement hire. Something was shifting here. They had called the meeting, not Sam, and he was gratified to see they were really taking the ball and running with it.

As they assembled in Sam's office, Craig again acted as spokesman. Placing several résumés in front of Sam, he announced, "These are the ones we feel should be interviewed. We'd like your okay to proceed to the next step."

Sam scanned the résumés, liking what he saw. "This is great work, guys," he told the men, and he suggested that they follow up with HR to make the appointments.

"Best-case scenario," Craig responded, "is we'll be able to get them through here and have a recommendation to you by the end of next week."

As they stood to leave, Sam also stood and said, "I'm really proud of the way you all have handled this. I was dreading having to find somebody to replace Jerry, but you took that monkey off my back, and I'm grateful."

The supervisors were still for a moment, taking in Sam's words. Their boss had always given credit where credit was due, but this morning he'd showed a new level of appreciation. It felt new for Sam, too—and they all knew it. Everyone was smiling now, and the guys headed out the door and back to the warehouse floor.

Sam sat down, thinking about empowerment. If they could handle this, what else might they be able to do if he'd only let them? He saw the burden he'd been under for years, believing that he had to come up with all the ideas. Clearly, his guys had ideas. Ideas that could help the company grow. Sam felt a lightness that exceeded the pounds he'd dropped.

As he left work Friday afternoon, he had a profound feeling that whatever issues had gone unsolved that week would stay on his desk until Monday. Everything was moving in the right direction. Replacement of Jerry was underway. Nick was cooking up a plan to get their fulfillment numbers up. Time to relax and enjoy the weekend. Even the rush hour traffic wasn't a bother. He flicked on the radio and let some soft jazz work its way into him.

When Sam got home, Linda reminded him that it was their turn to host Third Saturday, a dinner group they'd formed some years ago with two other couples. The couples showed up the next evening, covered dishes in hand, and the group had a fine time of food and conversation on the patio.

Later, after their guests had left, Linda told Sam that one of the other women, Maxine, had noticed Sam's new slimness. Sam chuckled, saying it was probably just the light. "No, honey," his wife said, "it wasn't her imagination." She added, "You know what I noticed?"

Unsure what was coming next, Sam said, "Okay, I'll bite."

"You're less stressed. I used to feel like part of you was still in the warehouse. Tonight, I felt like you were really here."

Sam smiled. There was nothing to say. He slipped his arm around her waist and drew her close. Then they went back to cleaning up.

Sam drove eagerly to work on Tuesday. He was looking forward to his second coaching session with Nick, where Nick would present his plan for the process improvement. However, he didn't let his eagerness prevent him from being properly prepared. He took care of some details, checked in with his guys, and then sat down at his desk to review.

Taking out the action plan, he read and reread it, along with the notes he had taken during Nick's previous coaching session. The review proved to be a good reminder of the differences in their behavioral styles—something Sam would need to be conscious of during the coaching session. He'd need to listen, not be too talkative, and allow Nick to get everything out on the table. Sam knew these things didn't come naturally to him, so he went back to the field guide, brushing up on the best ways to flex his own style to complement Nick's.

Nick showed up a full ten minutes early for their appointment. Thinking that the old Sam would have kept him waiting, Sam immediately welcomed Nick into his office. Sam could tell Nick was excited and also a little scared, much like he'd felt the morning he drove off to his *Coaching to Win* workshop. He offered Nick a can of Grape Crush—Nick's favorite beverage—from the small fridge behind his desk. Nick cracked opened the can and, before Sam could even ask, launched into his plan to change the order fulfillment process.

"Okay, as you know, we get our orders from one hundred and twenty dealers," Nick began, a little out of breath. Sam nodded. "The way it's set up right now," he continued, "the guys come in, grab their orders and fill them. That means they could walk across all hundred and fifty aisles in the warehouse to fill a single order!"

Sam could hear the passion in Nick's voice. And he had certainly put his finger on a big part of the problem. The question was, would Nick be able to pinpoint a solution? It was a question that Sam dearly wanted to ask, but he reminded himself that his role was to listen, so he nodded again and allowed Nick to continue.

"So our guys are all over that warehouse throughout the day, picking orders. When they're done, they box them up and give them to the shipping checkers who'll close them out. They could have half a dozen orders for the same dealer during the day, but each order goes out to that dealer in a separate box. Meaning that we ship multiple boxes to the same dealers every single day, costing us man hours, supplies, and shipping!"

Sam was smiling now. Nick's assessment was right on. He'd pinpointed the problem areas. "So what's the solution?" he asked Nick.

Already on the edge of his seat, Nick inched even further out. "What if we have somebody batch the orders every morning?" Getting only a nod from Sam, he went on. "We assign each guy a zone in the warehouse that consists of, say, five to six aisles. They become responsible for filling the portion of the order that falls within their zone. Then they take it to a bin designated for that dealer."

What if. Sam saw the magic in those two simple words. *The old me would have probably gotten defensive,* he thought, remembering his own hand in the current order fulfillment process. But here was a new idea. The day had arrived for him to become part of the solution. But he had to focus. Nick was moving on.

"As each dealer's bin fills, the shipping checkers box it up and ship it out. And here's the benefit. Doing it this way, everyone will get to know and own his or her zone. They will be responsible for keeping it cleaned and stocked. That should decrease the number of times we can't fill an order because we ran out of parts. They won't be running all over the warehouse any more. They'll just pull from their own area." Nick assessed whether Sam was with him. He summarized by saying, "We don't waste time and money shipping multiple boxes with only one or two parts to each dealer. We can combine the shipments, saving money on both boxes and shipping, and the shipping checkers will be able to close out earlier because they don't have as many boxes to handle."

Nick hesitated, then added, "Okay, I guess that's a lot. What do you think?"

Sam was thinking, but not about Nick's question. As Nick was giving the details of his process improvement ideas, Sam couldn't help thinking that Nick had been working this out in his head for a long time—much longer, in fact, than the week since Sam had handed him the challenge. How long had he known there was a solution but kept it to himself?

Sam snapped back into the moment and saw Nick staring at him. "Well, I like it," Sam weighed in cautiously, "but can you clarify a couple things for me?" He then questioned Nick on some specifics of the new process, and found the answers satisfactory. Mentally, he was already buying into Nick's idea. He could imagine the whole thing working quite well.

He had a bigger question for Nick, however, and now was the time to ask it. "Something became clear when you were pitching me on this. You've been thinking about this for a while, haven't you? Much longer than since we met about it last Tuesday."

Nick shrugged and replied a little sheepishly, "Well, yeah, I guess I have been thinking about it for quite a while."

His suspicion now confirmed, Sam pressed on. "So why didn't you say anything? You're telling me you had this great idea, and you just sat on it?"

Feeling like he was on the ropes, Nick shot back, "Why? Because you never asked me!"

The reply landed on Sam like a boxcar. He'd never asked. And that was true. He'd been the one with all the ideas, and his guys were there to execute on those ideas. But now he saw that Nick could have ideas too, ideas that could save time and money. Sam felt a wave of anger and embarrassment. How much company time and money had he wasted, failing to recognize the talent that lived right under his nose?

Nick's voice brought him back into the room. "Sorry, Sam," Nick said in a conciliatory tone. "I just never thought you were interested. So I kept my trap shut and did what I thought you were paying me to do."

There was an awkward silence. Sam knew he needed to rally. Whatever had happened in the past was now in the past. What mattered was how they went forward. His anxious face broke into a grin. "Well, Nick, that was the old regime. I'm sorry I failed to see what a talented guy you are. It scares me that if we hadn't begun this coaching thing, I might never have found that out."

Nick, relieved, was smiling too. "No problem, boss," he said cheerily. "What do we do next?"

Grateful that the conversation was moving on, Sam said, "So now we have a plan. How are you going to implement it?"

"Well, I think I'd meet with the other supervisors first," Nick responded, "and together we'd work out a way to put all this into action. I doubt there will be much pushback, Sam. We've actually been kicking this thing around over lunch for quite a while now."

Amazement showed on Sam's face. The solution to their lagging numbers had been there all the time. He felt like kicking himself. What other ideas did these guys have for improving the place that had never made it to his desk, all because he never asked?

"This meeting has been very informative," Sam said with a chuckle. "How soon do you think you can meet with the other supervisors and get this in the works?"

Standing, Nick replied, "It's done, boss. I'll go gather them right now." He was walking briskly toward the door when Sam interrupted his exit.

"Oh, and Nick—if you ever have a great idea like this again and don't share it with me, you're fired!"

Nick turned and smiled. "Understood, boss. Or you could just start talking football around me again."

Sam sat for a moment, taking it all in. Part of him wanted to dwell on the past, to wonder what life would have been like if he'd instituted this kind of change five years ago. Brushing it aside, he reminded himself that there was a time and a place for everything, and the time for this was now. Not five years ago.

Looking ahead, he felt a surge of excitement. He was sitting on a gold mine, a group of talented guys who only needed a little enabling in order to shine. He was on the cusp of something big, and he knew it. He'd get their initiative revved up. There would be no stopping them, no end to what they might accomplish together.

Sam wished the conference call with Scott were today. He couldn't wait to share with his colleagues his meeting with Nick and all that had transpired. But there was work to be done.

In fact, the next two days passed quickly. On Thursday, Sam was at his desk, dialing in to the conference call. His assignment was done, and he was eager to relate his progress. He reviewed his second coaching with Nick, seeing again how preparation and asking the right questions had helped him succeed.

Once the group was connected, Scott led them through the week's learning piece from the field guide. Sam was proud of how his concentration had grown. The idea of multitasking during these calls didn't even enter his mind now. When Scott asked them to share about their coaching sessions, Sam jumped in but was a little disappointed when another participant grabbed the floor first. He knew he'd get his turn, so he listened with interest while the colleague described her coachee's plan for trimming days off their month-end close.

As the dialogue went on, Sam realized that the speaker was Lana, the person who'd had a tough start the last time around, admitting that she hadn't done her preparation. "I've got to be honest. I wasn't really into any of this," Lana confessed. "But when I saw the difference between the outcome of my previous coaching session and this one, I guess I'm a believer now. A little homework beforehand, thinking through what I was going to say, made a world of difference."

"Welcome aboard, Lana!" Scott said warmly, and a muffled cheer went up from many of the participants. "And it doesn't really matter that you got here a week late," Scott went on. "The important thing is that you got here. Let's be honest. Often there's a lot of pressure on you all. The people at the top expect you to be expert coaches of your direct reports. Until you acquire the skills, it's hard to meet that expectation. But once you do, your frustration turns into motivation. You begin to feel like there's nothing you can't do."

What followed was more of the same—other newly minted coaches sharing similar progress with their coachees. Sam finally got in on the tail end of the discussion, telling of his Tuesday session with Nick and his realization about the untapped talent right under his nose. "I was pretty humbled by it," he said. "I used to think it was up to me to come up with all the ideas. Frankly, it's a little hard to give that up. But it's also a big relief. Knowing that I have guys willing and able to step up and take on new challenges is an amazing feeling. Now when I retire in a few years, I know I'll be leaving things in good hands."

Scott closed out by asking if there were any questions. Sam heard a familiar voice jump in. It was Chris, his role-playing partner from the *Coaching to Win* workshop. "Hey, Scott, I'm just wondering," Chris began. "Since I started working with my coachee, word has gotten around. Now I have another one of my direct reports—a really sharp guy named Vince—asking me if he will get this coaching too."

"That's great!" replied Scott. He reminded the group that when they completed phase 3 of the training with their current coachees, their responsibility would be to coach all of their direct reports. "Tell Vince for now that you appreciate his asking, and that he's a little ahead of the curve. Tell him that you're still in training, and in just a few more weeks, you'll be able to start coaching him too.

"I'm glad Chris brought that up." Scott addressed the participants. "Word does tend to get around, so you need to be prepared. You can take my advice to Chris and apply it to your own situations as they arise. The main thing is to not lose their enthusiasm. Let them know it's coming, and you're looking forward to coaching them as well."

As Scott finished up the call, he reminded them to complete next week's learning assignment in the field guide and conduct the third session with their coachee. Good-byes were said, and Sam pressed the button on his phone, disconnecting himself from the call.

Sitting silently at his desk, he gave himself a moment to reflect on all that had happened in the last few weeks. Sam couldn't get over the degree to which he seemed to be taking all this in stride. With Jerry's departure, everyone was taking up the slack. What was different, he realized, was that no one was grumbling anymore. He smiled when he thought back to that first meeting with his warehouse supervisors. Getting their input and making them part of the solution had made all the difference.

Friday afternoon came around, and Sam was back at his desk. Having cleared the decks, he found himself with time to begin the learning assignment for the following week. Bent over his field guide, he was surprised to glance up and see Reggie standing in his doorway.

"TGIF?" Reggie asked, reluctant to interrupt Sam's reading.

"Hey, Reggie!" Sam shot back enthusiastically. "Come in!"

Reggie remained in the doorway. "Sorry, can't stay but a second. Executive committee has had me lassoed in planning meetings for the last three days. Got to catch up on the backlog. Just wanted to say 'hey.'"

Sam hid his disappointment. There was so much he wanted to tell Reggie—about the workshop, his coaching of Nick, Nick's process improvement plan, and the way his guys were taking the lead in hiring Jerry's replacement. However, now was not the time. He'd have plenty of opportunities to fill Reggie in later. Reggie looked tired.

Sam saw something else too. Before, whenever Reggie had shown up at his door, Sam had always felt a little nervous, fearing he might have dropped the ball on something. Not today. Today there was nothing but good news in the warehouse. And it could wait.

Turning to go, Reggie paused, saying, "You been working out, Sam?"

Sam laughed out loud. "Optical illusion," he assured his boss, and a moment later Reggie was gone.

Sam had given Nick some space that week to begin implementing his plan. It was the right strategy. He was curious to know how things were going, but having Sam hovering like an expectant father was the last thing Nick needed. He'd find out soon anyway, as their next coaching was coming up Tuesday. Sam shut down his computer, signaling the official start of the weekend.

The broad sky above the Illinois plain was flawlessly blue as he pulled onto the parkway for the trip home. There were still plenty of challenges to be met. Nick had come up with a great idea. On paper. Sam hoped it would play out but knew they had a long way to go. And even if it was feasible operationally, would it do the trick? Would it move the needle enough get their fulfillment numbers up to an acceptable level?

Sam had gotten better at not taking work problems home with him. But this one was tougher to shake. It felt like so much was riding on the success of Nick's idea, for Nick and for himself. The whole thing was public by now. If it worked, there would be kudos all around, and Sam's reputation as a coach would be secured. If it flopped—well, he didn't even want to think about that scenario. There was one thing worse than death in Sam's book, and that was public embarrassment.

Impulsively, he detoured off the main drag and headed to a florist in the heart of downtown. Minutes later, he emerged with a dozen long-stemmed yellow roses. They were Linda's favorite. She was his Texas girl, born and raised. Sam was, by his own admission, a reluctant romantic. But Linda had stuck by him, and the last year had been a little bumpy. Today was as good a day as any to say thanks.

"Everything okay?" Sam heard his wife's voice from upstairs. The flower run had made him twenty minutes later than usual. Coming down, Linda was surprised to see her husband at the bottom of the stairs, roses in hand. "Did you wreck the car?" she asked, receiving the beautiful blooms and pressing her nose to the soft petals.

"No, of course not!" Sam replied.

Her eyes were wet as she hugged him. In her tears, he saw that there hadn't been nearly enough roses in their marriage. But that could change too. There was a time and a place for everything. And the time for roses was now.

Your Turn to Win: You've identified your coaching objective and measure of success. You've considered the relationship you already have with your coachee. Your next step is to plan your first coaching dialogue. Two tools will help you through this process.

1. **The Three *Ps***—An effective coaching dialogue begins with thoughtful opening statements. A helpful tool to plan opening statements is the "Three *Ps*" approach:

    *   Purpose—the reason for your discussion
    *   Process—how you and your coachee will interact during the discussion
    *   Payoff—the benefits for your coachee, for you, and for the company

Using the Three *P*s approach, take a moment to craft your opening statement for your first coaching session:

2. **Know/Do/Feel**—Another tool to plan an effective dialogue is the Know/Do/Feel method, which involves asking yourself the following questions:

    *   Know—What do I want this coachee to know?
    *   Do—What do I want this coachee to do?
    *   Feel—What do I want this coachee to feel?

Take a moment now and answer these questions for your upcoming coaching session:

Chapter Seven
THE UPSET

Monday, 7:50 a.m.

A gray sky stretched from one side of the windshield to the other as Sam headed in for work. The forecast from the car radio had said nothing about rain. Cloudy or not, it didn't change Sam's enthusiasm. He couldn't wait to grab his morning coffee and check out the lines-per-man-hour report from Friday that would offer proof that Nick's process improvement idea was having an impact on their numbers.

Coffee in hand, he settled into his chair to digest the good news. Funny, that chair had been squeaking less of late. Saturday's weigh-in at home had revealed he'd shed another two pounds.

Sure that the report would offer good news, Sam paused before double-clicking to open the file. Words were rolling around in his head, the congratulatory speech he'd deliver—first to Nick, then to the rest of his warehouse supervisors.

What the report showed, however, brought Sam's celebration to an abrupt halt. Had there been a glitch in the tabulation? Friday's lines per man hour were lower than they had been in months.

Sam reread it, letting out a sigh. How could this be true? He wanted answers, and fast. Grabbing the phone, he paged Nick to his office.

Minutes passed. Sam drummed his fingers impatiently on the desktop. He paged again. Finally, Craig buzzed in. "Hey, Sam. I heard you paging Nick. Dentist appointment—he'll be in late. Anything I can do you for?"

"No," Sam replied curtly. "Just tell him to see me when he gets in."

70

Sam rubbed his eyes. Fishing out the notes from his last coaching session with Nick, he searched for reasons. This should have worked. The process improvement idea was sound. And Sam had been clear that Nick should enlist the other warehouse supervisors and get the ball rolling right away. What could have gone so wrong?

Sam experienced a powerful instinct—to grab the ball, put Nick on the sidelines, and make this work. As he reached for the phone to call Craig up to his office, he stopped himself. This was Nick's plan. It was up to him to make it work.

Sam sat back, took a deep breath, and reached for his coffee. He would need to think carefully about how to handle the conversation with Nick. Taking out his action plan, he made some notes.

The dental appointment was providential. It had prevented a knee-jerk reaction on Sam's part. He spent the next twenty or so minutes trying to structure their next interaction.

A half hour later, Sam looked up to find Nick at his door. The right side of his jaw was slightly swollen. Nick pointed to it, mumbled "Novocain," and flopped down in the chair opposite his boss.

Sam got right to the point. "Nick, I'm a little concerned about these numbers." He handed Nick Friday's report. "They seem to be dropping instead of getting better."

Silence followed. Something told Sam he should keep his mouth shut and listen. The silence soon broke as Nick unloaded—a torrent of angry complaints about the guys down in the warehouse. Nick was talking so fast and his speech was so distorted by the numb jaw that Sam finally waved his arms, practically shouting, "Hey, Nick, calm down! It'll be okay."

When Nick regained his composure, Sam calmly ventured, "Why don't you take me back to the beginning?"

Point by point, Nick took Sam through what had transpired since their last meeting. "I went right out of here last week and got the other supervisors together," he began. "No problem getting them on board. Like I told you, we've been talking about this thing forever. So they called their guys together and told them about the changes we wanted to make."

Nick paused. Sam had an inkling of what was coming next, but sat quietly, waiting for Nick to continue.

"That's where it all fell apart," Nick fumed, his anger rising back to the surface. "I don't know what the deal is. These guys have been complaining since day one about the old process. But when we started talking about changing it, I guess they figured management was somehow out to get them. And when their supervisors told them these changes were nonnegotiable, it was like throwing gas on the fire. Oh, they went through the motions of making the change, but at about half the normal speed. It was a real slowdown. And the numbers reflect it."

Nick was completely dumbfounded by their behavior. "What's with these guys? We give them a chance to make their jobs easier, and they get caught up in some fantasy about management being out to get them, that it's only a ploy to cut the head count here and make those who are left work even harder!" Steam was coming from Nick's ears. He winced and rubbed his jaw. "Maybe we should just forget the whole thing," he declared, slouching even lower in the chair.

The two sat silently. Sam wanted to make sure that Nick had emptied his tank before Sam spoke. "I get your frustration. As I listened to you, I was feeling a little déjà vu. Can you guess why?"

Nick, who hardly seemed in the mood to play guessing games, remained quiet. It was the opening Sam had been looking for.

"I was in your same spot when I called you guys in for that first meeting to discuss Jerry's replacement. Remember?" There was a glint of recognition in Nick's eyes. "Like you, I had it all worked out—the perfect solution. But you guys acted like you'd been hit with a bucket of water."

A smile played across Nick's face. He clearly remembered the meeting well.

Sam went on to tell Nick how he had turned things around using Reggie's advice. "That's when I learned 'People are more likely to support that which they help create' isn't just an empty phrase," Sam said. "Do you remember what happened the second time? We had another meeting—an instant replay—only this time, I asked for your feedback."

"And you invited Jerry," Nick added. "And I thought you weren't going to use those football terms around me anymore." But Nick was smiling.

"I get it," Nick admitted, sitting up a little. "I guess I thought I had the perfect plan, and it was so hard to watch it go down in flames." He was quiet for a moment and then asked, "Do you really think getting input from the warehouse guys can salvage this thing?"

"Well," said Sam with a grin, "there is no such thing as a sure thing, but if it worked once, it will probably work again. Think of it this way. Like you, those guys have waited a long time to get a voice in how things are done around here. Give them that voice and they'll get on board. Let them modify your plan a little. It won't hurt. Just set some boundaries like I did. Let them know you're open to their ideas, but the final decision rests with you."

Nick hesitated; then he sprang out of the chair. "Got it, boss," he said and walked purposefully out of the room.

Sam sat nervously, unsure what to do next. Instinct told him to do something. But this was Nick's deal. And as frustrated as Nick had appeared, Sam knew that he was no quitter. He'd get back down in the warehouse and sort things out. Besides, Sam thought, his regular coaching with Nick was the next day. In a little more than twenty-four hours, he'd be able to gauge which way the wind was blowing, and the approximate velocity.

The rest of the day was a blur. Craig had sent a detailed e-mail on the preliminary interviews with candidates for Jerry's job. There were two whom Craig wanted to call back to meet with Sam. Sam gave his okay, suggesting they set something up through HR for the end of the week. There was Monday's usual mass of e-mail to be digested.

Sam also wanted to be ready for his coaching with Nick. Action plan in front of him, he revisited it in light of the day's events. He also went back to Nick's behavioral style assessment. The situation was pretty fluid right now. Sam knew success lay in his ability to flex his own style in a way that would make Nick feel supported but also motivated to find a solution.

By Tuesday afternoon, Sam was ready. Nick arrived at two on the dot, looking a little apprehensive but still in control. "Good news?" Sam asked, offering him a Grape Crush and a chair.

Nick frowned. "Well, sort of," he replied. "When I left your office yesterday, I went straight to the other warehouse supervisors. First thing I felt like doing was letting them know how frustrated I was about the slowdown. But then I thought how, when I came in here yesterday, you just listened. You let me get it all out. Something told me they needed to do the same thing.

"They were as frustrated as I was," Nick continued. "Once we got all that out on the table, I decided to steal some more of your material." Nick grinned at Sam. "Like you did with me, I reminded them of that first meeting we had after Jerry gave his notice. They remembered how we all grumbled and stomped out of the room. Then I asked them to remember the second meeting, the one where you invited Jerry."

Nick had recalled for them how Sam's asking for their input had turned things around. Explaining how they'd made the same mistake rolling out their process improvement idea, Nick then proposed the solution. "First time, it was like we said, 'Okay, guys, here's this big change. Don't ask any questions. Don't think, just do it.' This time we need to do it right. We need to get their input. Tell them, 'It's a good plan, but it's not perfect.' We'll allow them to help us make it better."

Nick described the discussion that ensued. "They were a little worried about opening this up to suggestions. But I told them, just like you told me, that we have the final say. I also suggested we call a meeting with everyone to get their input. That way we send the message we're all a team in this, and they can't play the three of us against each other."

Sam was impressed. "That all sounds great," he said, "though your bit about 'teamwork' is awfully close to a sports analogy."

"Oh, don't even go there," Nick shot back with a chuckle. He sipped his soda.

"So how'd that team meeting go?"

Nick replied, "It may be a little early to tell. We did get everybody together yesterday afternoon and asked for their input. We even got the shipping checkers involved in setting up the dealer boxes and creating that part of the process." He thought for a moment. "I'm optimistic that we're at least on the right track. You could feel the whole mood change down there when we asked for their feedback. Of course, there are always skeptics—the ones who want to see you fail. But they're a tiny minority. Time will tell."

Nick went quiet. His eyes were on the lines-per-man-hour report that lay on the near corner of Sam's desk. "Hey, just out of curiosity, how often do you get those reports?" Nick inquired.

Sam picked up the piece of paper. "I get these every day," he replied. "To be honest, I don't always look at them every day. With the numbers where they are, it got to be a little discouraging."

"Okay, don't blow me out of the water right away on this," Nick said. "One thing I figured out is our warehouse guys are really competitive. If I could share these numbers with them every day, it might spark their competitive spirit." His lips formed a wry smile. "Kind of like the Bears and Rams, right? Everybody plays harder if they know the score?"

Sam suppressed a laugh. Here he'd been trying to flex his own style to complement Nick's, and Nick was figuring out how to do the same thing back at him. A current of pride raced through him as he understood what was happening. If Nick could come this far in only three coaching sessions, in a couple of months he would be unstoppable.

Suddenly Sam was enthusiastic. The obligation to eventually coach all of his direct reports had felt like a burden. Now, however, it felt doable.

Sam considered Nick's request. "I have to think about it," he told Nick finally. He wanted to run the idea by Reggie. "Let me check into it. Should be okay. I'll let you know tomorrow."

Sam glanced back at his notes. He was beginning to wrap things up, but there were still a couple things he needed to cover. "As far as those naysayers, remember that there isn't much out there you can do that will please everybody," Sam said. "Right now, your focus should be on process improvement, not perfection. Can you think of any other barriers to getting this new process going?"

Nick replied that nothing came to mind immediately, but he'd be on the watch for obstacles and would bring them to Sam if they arose.

"Also, I know yesterday you had a lot to get out when we met," Sam continued. "In the future, though, it's okay to bottom-line it for me.

Include what details you think are necessary, but it's all right to just hit the high points. I'm a smart guy—I can connect the dots. If I can't, I'll ask you to clarify. Okay with that?"

"No problem," Nick replied. "We'll get this thing cooking, don't you worry." Nick crumpled his soda can, popped it into the air, and made a perfect basket in the trash can behind Sam's desk. "Get into hoops at all?" he asked Sam over his shoulder as he strode out of the office.

Sam sat smiling. He was still processing what had just happened when Reggie appeared at his door. "Hey, Reggie, great timing!" Sam announced.

Reggie looked puzzled, so Sam offered him a chair and described Nick's idea for sharing the numbers with the guys on the warehouse floor.

He'd barely finished before Reggie exclaimed, "Love it! Make it happen." He added, "One thing you're finding out is that this coaching thing can be as good for you as it is for your coachee. You may not have picked up on it, but right now you had no problem giving Nick credit for a great idea. That wouldn't always have been the case, right?"

Sam knew Reggie spoke the truth.

Reggie went on, "There's an old saying: 'I can accomplish anything as long as I don't care who gets the credit.' You're proving that, Sam. Keep it up." And with that, he was gone.

When Nick arrived at his locker early the following morning, Sam was standing there, paper in hand. "Careful what you wish for," Sam said with a chuckle, handing Nick yesterday's lines-per-man-hour report.

"Sweet!" Nick said with enthusiasm. "Love it when a plan comes together." He told Sam of his intention to post the report on the bulletin board next to the time clock. "That way, everybody will be able to see it when they clock in."

Sam wished Nick luck. "Same time tomorrow?" he asked.

"You bet!" sang Nick, and they parted to begin the day.

One day later saw a similar scene on the warehouse floor. Sam handed Wednesday's report to Nick. As Sam went upstairs, Nick uncapped a fat green marker and wrote at the bottom of the paper:

↑2%

The following day, Nick took the latest lines-per-man-hour report and scrawled at the bottom:

↑3.5%

He was beginning to attract an audience. A handful of guys stood and watched as he carefully posted the update over yesterday's report, inserting the pushpin exactly into the previously made hole.

That day, Sam stuck around to watch. After Nick had posted the report, Sam pulled him aside. "So what's the deal with the green marker?" he asked.

"Psychology," Nick replied. "Ever hear of it?" The two men laughed. "I wrote the percentage of improvement over yesterday's number at the bottom of the report," Nick continued. "When I did that, the guys got curious. They began asking their supervisors what it meant. The supervisors explained, and word got around. Hard to keep a secret down here—news travels pretty fast.

"And that isn't all of it," Nick continued. He was really grinning now. "Come Monday at our safety meeting, I'm putting a challenge out there. If the guys can hit the challenge percentage I come up with by week's end, we'll buy pizza for everybody on Friday."

Sam felt his mouth hanging open. Mentally, he made a note to correct his earlier prediction: Nick was already unstoppable.

Rarely in his life was Sam speechless, but he was now. At last, he said, "That's great. I'm happy to pop for the pizzas myself. And maybe I can sweeten the pot a little. If they make that goal Friday, I'll ask Linda to bake up some of her famous snickerdoodles."

He couldn't wait for Thursday's call with Scott and the other coaches. When they were all connected, Scott powered through the learning assignment and then asked the participants to share what had happened since last week.

Lana was first to jump in. She thanked the group for their encouragement, joking that it had felt like "tough love" at the time, but she had taken it to heart. Taking time to prepare was making an enormous difference in the outcome of her coaching sessions.

Others chimed in, anxious to share both their successes and random bumps in the road. Sam listened, wondering how to talk about his week with the group. It had been a real roller coaster, starting with Nick's tirade Monday, and developing into the upward trend in the numbers. The improvement was nothing to brag about yet, but small progress was better than none.

Sam's mind wandered to the weekend ahead. It would be good to leave all this behind for a couple of days. The turnaround had been stressful. He thought about what they were trying to do. Change in any organization was difficult. Sam had always been up for a challenge, but he knew that not everybody got excited about change. Some of those warehouse guys had been there a long time. To adopt a whole new way of doing things on the promise that it would make their lives easier could be hard to swallow.

Out of that reflection, Sam became aware that Scott was addressing him. "What about you, Sam? You've been pretty quiet today. Everything okay?"

Sam took a breath and then launched in. Remembering his advice to Nick, he tried to hit just the high points. He was pretty honest about his feelings, about how he'd wanted to grab the reins and fix things himself when they were heading south. He ended by describing Nick's creative way of challenging the workforce by posting the previous day's numbers and offering the pizza reward system.

When he finished, the phone line was silent for several moments. Clearly his story had had an impact on the listeners. It didn't feel odd, however. He hadn't been grandstanding. He'd been blowing Nick's horn, not his own.

Scott finally spoke up. "Okay, Sam, level with us. Prior to this whole *Coaching to Win* thing, did you have any idea that Nick was capable of all that?"

Sheepishly, Sam had to admit that he'd had no idea.

"It's all right," Scott said in a reassuring tone. "True, Nick's a talented guy. But your coaching was what really brought that gold to the surface. I think you deserve to pat yourself on the back." Sounds of affirmation blared from the speakerphone. His colleagues agreed; he had been an important part of this.

On Friday morning, the number of guys at the time clock had grown to about a dozen. Sam stood by as Nick took Thursday's report, wrote in green at the bottom, and pinned it over the top of yesterday's number.

↑5%

As Nick backed away from the board, a murmur went around the assembly. Sam saw several of the warehouse crew high-fiving each other. A small cheer went up. More of the crew gathered, curious at the commotion. The game was on.

Your Turn to Win: Before each of your coaching sessions, take time to fully prepare. Use the acronym below to help focus and guide you in the right direction.

C	Create a setting for coaching
O	Open-ended questions
A	Active listening
C	Collaborate and confirm
H	Help and encourage

1. **Create a Setting for Coaching**—Choose a setting that makes your coachee feel comfortable—a place where you both can completely focus on the discussion. Identifying a good setting also involves mental preparation on your part to ensure you can give your coachee your full attention. Decide which venue will put your coachee at ease and facilitate your objectives. How will you block interruptions like phone calls and walk-in visitors?

2. **Open-ended Questions**—The best time to decide what you are going to say is *before* you start speaking. Asking questions allows people to discover for themselves what you wanted to tell them. What open-ended questions will you use to engage your coachee? Remember the adage Reggie shared with Sam:

   **People are more likely to support
   that which they help create.**

With that in mind, what questions can you ask your coachee to help him or her further refine the coaching objective?

3. **Active Listening**—This means being completely tuned in to your coachee—listening to tone of voice and body language, as well as the spoken words. This type of listening demonstrates respect and understanding. What behaviors can you demonstrate (things your coachee can see or hear you say) that will communicate you are actively listening? Think about taking notes, paraphrasing, asking questions, etc.

4. **Collaborate and Confirm**—John Maxwell said it best: "Collaboration is multiplication!" Outcomes and goals should be clearly defined and mutually agreed upon by the coach and the coachee. Setting outcomes, objectives, and goals should be a collaborative process that involves dialogue.

Consider the following steps:

- Get Them Involved—A person is much more likely to be committed to achieving an outcome or goal if he/she is involved in setting it.
- Be SMART—Often goals can be expressed in SMART terms (specific, measurable, achievable, relevant, time-bound).
- Set Expectations—Ensure your expectations are absolutely clear. People perform at a higher level when they clearly understand what is expected of them.
- Clarify Outcomes—Make sure you and your coachee agree on the outcome or deliverable. Identify the WIIFM (what's in it for me) and WIIFY (what's in it for you).
- Be Flexible—Remember that you must pace the development with what your coachee is able to accomplish. Goals should be challenging, but not so stringent that performance suffers in other areas.

Jane Pierce

How do you plan to collaborate and confirm with your coachee?

5. **Help and Encourage**—Great coaches regularly help and encourage
    people around them by expressing support and belief in them. This
    may come naturally or it may take considerable effort. Regardless,
    it is important to integrate help and encouragement into your daily
    leadership and coaching activities.

How will you help and encourage your coachee throughout your
coaching engagement?

Chapter Eight

THE UPTICK

Monday, 7:35 a.m.

The sun streamed through a scattering of clouds as Sam drove to work. Traffic was moderate on the expressway this morning. He felt rested. His weekends had evolved from two days of work worries to a complete unwinding. Saturday morning, he'd made pancakes for Linda from scratch. The ritual dated from their newlywed days but had fallen off in recent years. Now it was getting reinstated, to the delight of them both.

All week, Sam had eagerly been sharing with his bride the progress at the warehouse. As he told the story, he was as surprised as anyone that things were going so well. He was still kicking himself a bit for not having spotted Nick's potential earlier. However, as Linda was quick to remind him, the important thing was not when he discovered it, but that he had discovered it. And his coaching skills were getting more polished, helping Nick to stay engaged.

"I kind of got you into something," Sam confessed as he poured a little more syrup on his stack. "I hope it's all right."

Linda raised an eyebrow and then smiled. "I'm sure I can handle it," she replied.

He proceeded to tell her the details of the pizza challenge, and that he'd offered to sweeten the reward with her snickerdoodles.

"My gosh, Sam, I haven't made those in a month of Sundays!" she exclaimed. She figured they'd need about twelve dozen for all those guys. Sam promised to pick up the cookie ingredients before the weekend was out.

At two minutes before eight on Monday morning, he was standing at the time clock with Friday's lines-per-man-hour report in his hand, folded in half. Nick arrived a minute later. As Nick reached for the report, Sam playfully snatched it back. "What do you think? Take a guess!"

Nick's face showed worry. "Bad news?" he asked.

Feeling guilty, Sam handed over the paper and watched Nick's momentary distress turn to joy. The bottom line showed that not only were things still heading in the right direction, they were even picking up speed.

"Up 12 percent?" Nick said with a mix of pride and amazement. "How about that!"

When they had savored the moment, Sam said, "Okay, help me understand something. You got all this to happen just by putting up these numbers every day and promising your guys a round of pizzas?"

"Yeah, I know," Nick said humbly. "But it's really more than that. What we did was give these guys a chance to create it. Like you said, if they help create it, they're more likely to support it. So they're really proving that their ideas were the right way to go. They want to be seen like I want to be seen—as guys who bring value to this equation, not just workers who punch a time clock."

During the last moments of Nick's speech, the warehouse team had gathered around him. Overhearing what Nick was telling Sam, they nodded.

Walking back to his office, reality began to settle in for Sam. The early signs were good, but he wondered how they could sustain this progress. Buying the guys pizza every week wasn't feasible. And even if it were, he knew the effect would be short-lived. Pizza would not be enough to keep these guys engaged, to keep them reaching to beat the numbers week after week. Again, as he reminded himself, it was as much a question for Nick as for Sam. He settled into his desk chair, got out the action plan, and made notes on how he'd address the sustainability issue with Nick during their next coaching session.

A knock on the door made him look up. Reggie stood in the doorway, coffee in hand, wearing a big smile. Sam rose and offered his boss a chair.

"I just saw the numbers!" Reggie exclaimed. "What in the heck have you guys been up to?"

For Sam, this nearly opened the floodgate. He had so much he wanted to tell Reggie about Nick's process improvement and their progress. He paused, however, recalling that their behavioral styles were similar. There was a lot to tell, but Reggie was much like he was and didn't like to be buried by the details. Sam realized he could flex his style and make their interaction more successful.

Focusing on the main points, Sam took Reggie through the process, including the resistance they'd encountered initially from the warehouse guys, and how getting their input in the process improvement had overcome that hurdle. He shared Nick's challenge to the workforce of a 95 percent or better fulfillment rate.

Reggie cut in, suggesting that at their current pace, it seemed like they would hit that challenge number by the end of the week. "I'd like to see this thing in action," Reggie said, and the two men headed downstairs to the warehouse floor.

Walking the wide aisles stacked floor to ceiling with an array of bins, Reggie immediately sensed a change. "Is it just me," he ventured, "or did this place get cleaned up?"

Sam chuckled, explaining the strategy. "Each guy down here now gets his own area. Think of it like a zone defense. Before, there was no ownership. Now, each guy is responsible for his zone—for keeping it clean and stocked.

"It solved a lot of issues," Sam went on. "Before, it was easy to pass the buck if an area was dirty or poorly stocked. Like, 'It's not my problem.' Now, they've got pride because they own the territory. They take it very seriously."

Barry, one of the workers in the warehouse, approached and began pulling parts from a bin to fill an order. "Reggie, this is Barry, and this is his slice of the pie," Sam said. "Barry, Reggie is our regional manager." The men shook hands, and Sam described how Barry and the other guys had taken Nick's process improvement idea and offered suggestions that made it even better.

It was Reggie's turn to offer praise. "Barry, this is excellent!" he said. "I really appreciate your efforts. You guys are making a huge difference here." Barry gave a quick nod and went back to filling the order.

Walking on, Sam caught Barry smiling to himself. Barry was an old-timer. He'd been working on that warehouse floor as long as Sam could remember. Like Sam, he was nearing retirement. His response to Reggie's recognition seemed muted, but it occurred to Sam that it might have been the first time a regional manager from the company had even spoken to him, let alone given him a compliment. He realized that there was untapped talent here too. It was all over the place. And, thankfully for everyone, untapped no longer.

The tour continued as Sam took Reggie to the area where the bins designated for specific dealers were located. He explained the process. "Our shipping checkers monitor the orders and the bins, and they make sure the parts that have been picked match up with the order. When a bin is full, the order gets boxed and shipped out."

A pair of shipping checkers working in the area eyed them curiously. "Guys, this is Reggie, our regional manager," Sam said to them.

Shaking their hands, Reggie asked, "You think this is all a change for the better?"

Bruce, a tall man with graying sandy hair and powerful hands assured Reggie it was. He listed the benefits they'd experienced on the floor.

Reggie listened, his interest piqued when Bruce added, "On average, we're saving over $500 a day on boxes and almost $1,000 daily on our shipping costs."

Angie, Bruce's coworker, jumped in. "And here's another benefit. The new process now allows us time to actually recheck the orders before they go out. Since we started doing that, we haven't had a single call from a dealer being angry that we shipped the wrong part. Now they don't call us shipping checkers for nothing."

Sam could tell Reggie was doubly impressed. The cost savings and increase in dealer satisfaction were definite improvements. And they hadn't even mentioned the hidden cost savings—the money saved now that they weren't restocking wrong parts returned by the dealers, or the labor and mailing costs of correcting orders and sending them back out. Sam watched Reggie's face, imagining him calculating the annual cost savings in his head, multiplied across all the warehouses in the region. What he saw confirmed Sam's belief that they were on to something big.

As the pair walked briskly back to Sam's office, it was clear that Reggie had seen enough. "This is too good to keep to ourselves, Sam, don't you think?" he asked. Back in the office, Reggie's enthusiasm was in high gear. Eagerly, he described putting together a plan to roll out the process improvement regionally.

Sam listened to his boss, realizing all the while that something was missing from this picture. Or, better yet, someone: Nick. He remembered how the faces of the guys in the warehouse beamed as they talked with Reggie about the new process. Nick should be here to bask in the glory of it. Abruptly Sam said, "Excuse me," to Reggie, grabbed up his phone, and paged the warehouse.

Nick arrived five minutes later, immediately wary when he saw Reggie. It was a reality check for Sam. Nick's demeanor had changed so much over the course of their coaching sessions that he'd forgotten how easily his coachee could shut down at the first sign of danger. Clearly, Nick thought he was walking into an ambush.

In an instant, Sam's mind ran over everything he knew about Nick's behavioral style, searching for a way to help Nick through what was about to transpire. He blasted himself for his impulsiveness. He should have thought this through before summoning Nick, and he resolved not to make that mistake again.

Sensing that a preemptive strike might be best, Sam took the lead before his boss could speak. Offering Nick a chair and his security Grape Crush, he explained why their manager was there. He told of Reggie's discovery of the up-trend in their production numbers. Thinking ahead as he spoke, Sam recalled two important keys in Nick's behavioral style—he liked a challenge, but he wasn't the type for a great show of emotion, especially in the presence of a manager two levels above him.

The key to this, Sam realized, was underplaying it. The room had been teeming with excitement and emotion before Nick came in. The game now was to keep things calm and focused. Sensing Sam's shift, Reggie took over the lead, relating to Nick their recent warehouse tour. As he recounted this, he directed his praise at the warehouse workers and shipping checkers, but not directly at Nick. Sam could see Nick begin to thaw and relax a bit. It was time to pose the question.

"All this success is making the two of us wonder," Sam said, "if this process improvement might work in the other warehouses in the region." Knowing his coachee liked time to think things over, he kept talking. "Give it some thought and let me know. Maybe you want to kick it around with the other supervisors and then get back to us with a recommendation."

Nick was visibly more relaxed now and took a sip of his soda. The relief was evident on his face. He wouldn't have to commit himself right now.

In the silence that followed, the three men were all coming to the same conclusion. A lot was at stake here. Nick's recommendation could potentially impact operations for the entire region.

"Got it," said Nick, breaking the silence. "I'll ask the guys, sniff it out, and get back to you. When do you need an answer by?"

Sam glanced at Reggie and then replied, "Oh, a day or two. Let me know if you hit any obstacles. Take the time you need. It's important for all of us that if we choose to do this, we do it right."

"Sure thing, boss," Nick replied, rising to leave. In the office doorway, he raised his soda can in salute. "Thanks for the opportunity." He took one final swig, crunched the can, and strode out.

When Nick was out of earshot down the hall, Reggie laughed heartily and demanded, "Sam, who was that guy?"

Sam joined in the laugh. "Yeah, I know, right?"

Reggie wasn't a guy to regularly dole out praise, but this morning his praise for Sam was effusive. "You completely turned that around. Your guy came in here like a condemned man and left like a man who is standing on top of the world."

Sam received Reggie's praise but was quick to add, "Truthfully, I almost blew it. Our style is very different from Nick's. I'd forgotten that when I called him up here, so I had to adjust on the fly. Next time, I'll count to ten and think strategy before I go charging ahead."

"Well, I'll take off a half point for that," Reggie replied jokingly. "Remember, you're still learning, just like Nick is. By the time you get to coaching your other direct reports, you'll have this thing down."

Sam smiled, grateful for Reggie's kind words. But Reggie wasn't done.

"Can I be honest with you, Sam?" he asked. Sam nodded. "When I pitched you on doing this *Coaching to Win* thing, I wasn't sure you'd take to it. You're a lot like me. And I know how difficult it was for me. But from what I'm seeing, you're leaving me in the dust! I should be taking notes from you!"

It was Sam's turn to laugh out loud. When the laugh subsided, he said, "Thanks, Reggie. That means a lot." Sam thought for a minute. "Maybe we could trade tips, like when we see each other?" he offered. "The thing those once-a-week conference calls taught me is there's power in numbers. Being able to talk with others on a weekly basis, share not only where we hit the mark but also our misfires, really helps the lessons sink in."

"Great idea!" said Reggie.

The men agreed that whenever they met up, Sam would update Reggie on the progress of his coachees—there would soon be more than just Nick—and anything he had learned along the way.

Standing to leave, Reggie shook Sam's hand. "Keep it up," he said. "I have a feeling there's more gold lying around here, and you're clearly the guy to find it."

Now that Nick was picking up speed, Sam firmly resolved to be prepared for all their interactions. First thing Tuesday morning, he pulled out his action plan to get ready for their afternoon coaching session. Happily, he wasn't starting from scratch. He'd gotten in the habit of jotting quick notes throughout the prior week to help build an agenda. At the top of the list was discussing Nick's plan for sustaining the process improvement in the long term.

Sam got so engrossed in his planning that he almost missed the eight o'clock morning ritual. Grabbing the latest lines-per-man-hour report from his printer tray, he made double time downstairs, where Nick was already waiting at the clock. As Sam approached, he began tapping his foot in mock impatience. "Where have you been?" Nick demanded. "Time is money!" Sam laughed and handed Nick the report.

The crowd for this morning ritual was growing. They circled around as Nick readied his green marker. Sam noted the confidence on Nick's face. It was like he knew without even looking at the new report that the numbers were up again. Marker in hand, he wrote in bold strokes and pinned the report over yesterday's figure.

↑15%

A cheer went up, mixing with the sound of many hands high-fiving the news.

Walking back up to his office, Sam heard someone calling his name. He stopped and turned around to find Nick running to catch up with him. "Hey, Sam," Nick began, a little out of breath, "you got a sec for me?"

Sam replied immediately, "Sure, anytime."

The two proceeded silently toward Sam's office. During their walk, Sam was tempted to break the silence. He was curious to know what was up that couldn't wait for their afternoon session, but he knew it was best to let Nick lead the discussion.

He didn't have long to wait. Even before they were seated, Nick blurted out flatly, "I don't think we're ready for a big rollout of this process improvement thing."

Sam waited for what would follow.

Nick went on to describe the bugs they were still trying to work out. "And then there's the issue of how to keep the momentum going on this after all the pizza's been digested."

Sam listened. He showed no surprise at Nick's statements. Nick was a cautious guy, and Sam had almost expected this. He looked down at the action plan that was still out on his desk and made a small check mark by his note about how to sustain the plan. He was pleased that Nick was already thinking about it.

Something then occurred to him about Nick's demeanor. During their conversation, Nick had avoided eye contact with Sam completely, instead looking first at his own hands and then down to the floor. He'd also been talking at about twice his normal rate. Sam realized that Nick had been nervous about telling him he didn't feel they were ready. It was time to put Nick at ease.

"I think you're 100 percent right," Sam said. "Let's not jump the gun. We want to do this right."

As Nick processed Sam's words, he gradually relaxed. He looked like he was now actually sitting in the chair instead of hovering above it. Nick continued the conversation by giving Sam some specifics on the bugs they were trying to work out of the new process. Sam made more notes and reminded Nick that they could discuss these further in their afternoon session.

The wry smile returned to Nick's face. "Can I tell you something?" he asked.

Sam nodded.

"You know that thing about killing the messenger? I was honestly afraid to come in here and tell you I didn't think we were ready to expand this to other warehouses. When I saw how sold you and Reggie were on the whole thing, I figured that the decision had already been made. I'd be scared to go against one manager, let alone two at once."

Sam smiled, showing that he understood. "I can see where you might have thought that, Nick, but we really did want your opinion. And I get how hot Reggie is on this deal, and how he wants to move forward right away. My job is to slow him down so we do it right. Let me worry about that so you can focus on the job at hand."

It was what Nick needed to hear. However, their exchange was interrupted by the paging system; Nick was needed down in the warehouse. "It's lonely at the top," he quipped with a grin, rising to go. "Still on for this afternoon?"

Sam nodded, and Nick was out the door.

The encounter left Sam even more enthused about coaching Nick that afternoon. He reviewed his notes, made a few more, and went on to other matters.

Lunchtime crept around, and Sam ate at his desk—a Cobb salad with ranch dressing and a plum for dessert. He was eager to dig in deeper with Nick on how to sustain the process improvement. And he wanted to share more thoroughly how pleased Reggie was with their turnaround. Nick's good work was getting the attention of upper management, and rightly so. Nick had a lot to be proud of.

Right on time, Nick came in and took his chair, cracking open the soda that Sam had put out for him. Nick was a different man now. The nervousness he'd shown in their morning session had gone, and Sam could tell Nick was fully engaged again.

"I don't want to embarrass you right off the bat," Sam said, "but Reggie is really singing your praises around here. Maybe I should be looking for a new job." They shared a laugh at that, and Sam went on to describe his strategy for keeping Reggie in check. "I know he's really gung ho about this new process, but I'll get him to see the sense in slow-rolling the whole thing until we're convinced the bugs are gone and it has proven to be a long-term solution."

"Thanks," said Nick. "I still really believe in the way we're going. I just want it to be as near perfect as it can be before it gets out there."

Sam agreed and moved their discussion on to the next point. "Have you given any thought to how we keep this thing going? I mean, the pizza is great, but that won't last. We have to think long-term here."

"Agreed," Nick replied. "I'm still doing a little research on that. Thought it might be good to get a group together—some of the regular warehouse team, some of the shipping checkers—to give us some ideas. Their input is really important here. I don't want to second-guess what will motivate them. Like I said, they're closest to the work. Also, as I learned after the first time, if they help shape it, they'll help support it. It'll be at least partly their baby."

"I think that's really smart," Sam agreed. "We do need to keep the ball rolling, however. When do you think you'll have something from them?"

Nick sipped his soda. "I want to give them adequate time, because I only talked about it with them yesterday. How about we shoot for a week? I should have their ideas by our coaching session next week."

"That should be fine," Sam said. He glanced at his notes and realized that they'd covered the two most important points. Again, he encouraged Nick to bring up any obstacles that were standing in the way. "Well, I guess that's it," Sam said finally.

Nick stood to leave. "Oh yeah," he said, referring to a small slip of paper in his hand. "We're going to need about fifteen pizzas for tomorrow. Three plain cheese, four pepperoni, and seven special with no green pepper. Thick crust. And don't forget those cookies."

Sam looked directly at Nick. "So I guess now I'm taking food orders from my warehouse supervisor? What is happening here?" he said, feigning irritation. "Got any dry cleaning you need me to pick up too?"

Nick laughed, and Sam joined in. There had been a lot more laughter around this place lately, Sam thought. More laughter in the last five weeks than in the previous five years. It felt good to laugh.

Sam stayed late on Wednesday to get the day's lines-per-man-hour report. As he waited at his computer, he experienced a moment of doubt. What if they didn't make the goal? What if they'd eked everything out of this process improvement already and the numbers had topped out?

He held his breath and accessed the report. Scanning down, his eyes went straight to the bottom line. Unbelievable. They had actually exceeded their goal by almost four percentage points. Sam high-fived the air, sent the document to print, and grabbed his keys.

The drive in to work Thursday morning was one he'd remember for a long time. Nearly thirteen dozen snickerdoodles were carefully stacked in aluminum pans across the back seat, filling the car with the warm, irresistible smell of cinnamon. Linda deserved the Congressional Medal of Honor for all that. He made a mental note to call their travel agent. Maybe they could get away for a few days next month.

Sam had it all planned out. Before meeting Nick at the time clock with the report, he would put the cookies in the break room with a sign saying CONGRATS. It was perfect. The guys could enjoy a cookie with their morning coffee. But as he reviewed his plan, something seemed wrong. It rolled around in his mind, and at last he saw it. This was Nick's show, not his. Nick should be the one handing out the rewards.

He parked, and in two trips carried the cookies up to his office. Hurrying back downstairs, he met Nick at the time clock, handing him the report. "I called the pizza place yesterday. Everything will get delivered at eleven thirty. I also have the cookies up in my office. What would you like me to do with them?"

"Wow," Nick said, "that's awesome!" He informed Sam that he and the other supervisors had a plan for the celebration. They'd made their own sign. All they needed to fill in was the final number from the report.

The excitement shone on Nick's face, like that of a kid bounding downstairs on Christmas morning. The crowd that had gathered around the time clock this morning was larger than ever and buzzing with excitement. This was Nick's moment too, Sam realized. He gave Nick a thumbs-up and headed back to his office. Had he stayed, he would have seen Nick post the new number along with a large green smiley face he'd drawn underneath it. The whoop that went up traveled all the way back to Sam's office.

Preparing for his Thursday call with the *Coaching to Win* group, Sam tried to remember a time when he'd felt more buoyant than this. He smiled as he recalled Reggie's confession about being unsure if Sam would take to this coaching thing. Sam had taken no offense at the remark. To be honest, he hadn't been sure either.

The call got underway. As he customarily did, Scott led them through the learning assignment and into the questions. One of these asked how they were expressing support and encouragement of their coachees. Sam had a lot to share. The week prior had been a real demonstration of the power of support and encouragement. He jumped right in when Scott called for the group to respond. Surprising himself, Sam was also eager to relate the times when he'd almost blown it: the impromptu meeting with Nick and Reggie where Nick felt ambushed, and how Sam had thought about giving out the cookies instead of allowing Nick to have his moment in the sun.

But Scott was complimentary through it all. "You've learned the difference it makes when you prepare for these interactions," he told Sam. "You've also learned how to work on the fly, to still use the skills you've acquired here in the moment. It would be nice if we got a week to plan everything, but that's not always your reality. Things will come up. Use the tools. They will guide you to the right outcome."

Scott reminded everyone to go through the field guide in preparation for next week. There was extra material. "Give yourselves a little more time on this next section—you may need it." With that, there was a round of good-byes, and Sam hung up the phone. He jotted a note to look over that material this weekend.

Friday afternoon came, and Sam was restless. He caught up on his deskwork and decided to take a stroll around the warehouse. How many hundreds of times had he walked around that floor during his tenure? It was impossible to count. But lately there was something different. An energy. A spirit. Something you couldn't quite put into words, and Sam wasn't going to try. Orders were being filled. Sections were being restocked and tidied before the weekend. And there was smiling. So much smiling. It was like something had gotten into the water.

Something else caught Sam's attention. There was music.

At that moment, he felt a brush on his elbow from behind. He spun around to find Nick standing there, still grinning like that kid on Christmas.

"You like the music?" he asked. Sam nodded. Nick explained. "Remember we used to have that piped-in music forever? It was awful—made you feel like you were trapped in some elevator back in 1969. So I had this old stereo and a couple of big speakers left over from my headbanger days. I brought 'em in, and now the guys get to pick the music. We're evenly divided down here. The older guys like their metal bands; the younger guys are hooked on country. But we switch it up pretty often, so everybody stays happy. Happy workers, good productivity. Motivation is the name of the game."

Sam chuckled. "I can see I have a lot to learn," he said, "and apparently you're just the guy to teach me."

Nick was laughing too. It was all music to Sam's ears.

Your Turn to Win: Great coaches are highly observant and attuned to their coachees. At any given time, a coach has awareness of how people are progressing toward their goals.

Three Principles of Effective Observation:

- **Be Objective**—Progress, like performance, should be evaluated using reasonable, unbiased, observable, and tangible measurements.
- **Be Specific**—Progress (or lack of progress) should be accurately and clearly defined so that effective feedback can be provided.
- **Be Timely**—Create a balance between allowing sufficient time for progress to be made and stepping in soon enough to identify bad habits or misdirection.

1. **Observing**—How do you plan to observe progress with your coachee? Consider scheduling a meeting, observing actions/ behaviors, or conducting an informal conversation.

2. **Evaluation**—After observing progress, you need to evaluate that progress relative to the agreed-upon goals or expectations.

   - *On Track*—Ideally, your coachee is on track and moving forward with his/her goals. In this case, reinforcement, recognition, and support are the best things to offer.
   - *Off Track*—On the other hand, your coachee may be off track or not making adequate advancements toward a goal. In this case, evaluation and analysis need to be done to determine the cause.

What specifically will you look for to determine if your coachee is on track or off track?

3. **Taking Action**—Once you've observed and evaluated progress toward the goal, it's time to take action by either reinforcing or redirecting specific behaviors. What specifically do you want to reinforce or redirect? What behaviors have you observed that are either contributing to progress or getting in the way of it? How will you address these behaviors?

Chapter Nine

THE 100 PERCENT SOLUTION

Friday, 10:15 a.m.

Sam sat looking at the folder that lay on the desk before him. It contained paperwork from human resources detailing the job offer for Jerry's replacement. He chuckled, recalling that a couple months ago, replacing Jerry seemed impossible. Now they were about to extend an offer to their top candidate, Lois. Sam knew instinctively that she would be a great addition to the team.

Craig and Mike had handled the whole process like pros. It was no small miracle in Sam's mind, and he marveled at how little he'd had to do to make it happen. A little empowerment had gone a long way. If these guys could produce results like that on a wing and a prayer, how much more would they be able to contribute once Sam began to coach them more fully?

Suddenly the possibilities seemed endless. Sam's dream for leaving the place in capable hands when he retired was beginning to seem real.

The warehouse was still buzzing from yesterday's celebration. Whenever he went down to the floor, workers stopped him to say thanks for the pizza and Linda's snickerdoodles, which had apparently caused a near-riot. Angie said that Nick had instructed them, "Only two apiece until everybody gets some." But when the call came for seconds, the table was practically stampeded.

Sam thanked each of them for their efforts and encouraged them to keep it up, to keep reaching for the next level. He couldn't wait to tell Linda what a hit her cookies had been. Nick was clearly a man of character. Sam had chosen to let Nick give out the rewards, but from the workers' feedback, it was clear that, in the end, Nick had given credit for the eats to Sam. Sam had tried to stay low-key by letting Nick take the credit, but in doing so, the credit had made its way back to him anyway. It all felt good.

After lunch, Sam recalled Scott's reminder during last week's call to allow extra time for their final learning assignment. Their final assignment. He couldn't believe how the eight weeks had flown by. Pulling up the field guide on his screen, he hit the Print button, planning to take the material home and finish it over the weekend.

That evening after dinner, Sam sat at their new kitchen table, working on his assignment. The walls had been painted in Oasis Green, which gave a fresh, outdoor feel to the room. After starting the dishwasher, Linda joined her husband at the table. Sam looked up and took her hand.

"I couldn't help thinking," he began, "the nights we used to sit out here after supper with the boys, helping them with their homework." Linda smiled, silently joining in Sam's recollection. "Seems like everything goes so fast," he added wistfully, and shared his realization from earlier that day about how quickly the *Coaching to Win* program had gone.

"This was quite a week," Sam told her. For the next half hour, he described all that had taken place at the warehouse since Monday—the blooming of Nick's leadership skills, the achievement of their goal, the pizza and cookies, and the hiring of Jerry's replacement.

"That's wonderful! You finally found somebody for Jerry's job!" Linda said. "What's his name?"

Sam smiled. "It's Lois," he replied simply.

Linda's eyes widened. "I think that's terrific!" she exclaimed. Teasingly, she added, "Now that place will really start to run!" They laughed together.

Sam showed up Monday wondering about the report. Thursday had not been a normal day in the warehouse. The celebration had been great but was also distracting. Still, he had high hopes that the upward trend in the numbers would continue. Fortunately, his hopes were not disappointed. Friday's lines-per-man-hour report showed that the process improvement had reached 97 percent. Sam sent up a silent cheer and then sent the report to print.

Waiting at the tray, he was both elated and a little concerned. They'd met the challenge, but now came the tough part. How could they keep riding the wave of this thing as the pizzas faded into memory? He studied the report more closely now, noticing that there were a couple of parts that always seemed to be on back order, keeping their fulfillment stats from going even higher. He resolved to check in with Nick on that this morning.

Handing Nick the report at the time clock, Sam sensed his coachee's frustration. *What now*? he thought. His wondering was cut short as Nick said, "Hey, can you sit down with me, Mike, and Craig sometime this morning? We've got an issue with these back orders and want to sound you out on a solution."

Sam told Nick he was free now, and the four men soon gathered upstairs in his office.

Nick started by passing the report back to Sam. At the bottom, he had written two numbers: CV2Z9F497B and BRRF-88.

"Those mean anything to you?" Nick inquired.

Sam studied the numbers. They seemed familiar. "I know they are parts numbers. Do I get a point for that? Couldn't tell you exactly what parts, though—it has been a while since I worked with the actual parts numbers."

Nick jumped in. "They're both parts for one of our most popular SUVs," he said. "The first is an engine sensor, and the other is a right front brake rotor. We get a lot of calls for both of these, and they're always stuck on back order."

Nick was speaking excitedly, and Sam knew he was eager to spring a solution on his boss. Sam nodded and kept listening.

Nick continued, "We all want to see if we can hit 100 percent fulfillment, but we have got to solve the problem on these back orders to hit that number. It's going to take some work, but I think we may have a solution. That's what we want to run by you."

Sam looked at his supervisors and smiled. He felt as excited as Nick now. Not so long ago, problems came from all over the warehouse to land on his desk. Today, he had three men in his office presenting not just the problem, but a solution. The refrain from that classic Dylan ballad rambled through Sam's head. The times, they were a-changing.

Sam flipped his attention back as Nick laid out a possible solution. "We've got an idea that we could network with other warehouses in the region to find those back-ordered parts. It will take a little work and maybe a little sweet-talking, but we think we can make it happen. Or at least it's worth a try. Besides, if we intend to roll this process improvement out to all the warehouses in the region, it's smart to start building those connections, get everybody on the same team."

Sam cracked a smile at Nick's sports analogy, but a quick look from his coachee said, "Don't even go there," so he fixed his face.

"I'm really impressed with you guys," Sam said. "You have my okay, and I'll let Reggie know the plan. Give me a holler if you get hung up anywhere." With that, the men hurried out of Sam's office.

Sam went back to work. He'd finished his homework—the coaching skills self-assessment—over the weekend. He'd seen firsthand the dramatic progress Nick and those around him had made. But he wondered, *Where do I stand? Am I really a better coach than when I started this whole thing eight weeks ago?*

He examined his field guide from the first phase of the program and ran down the areas where he initially had low scores. What pleased him was that he had racked up improvements in every one of those areas.

It made Sam truly happy to see his progress. Of all that he was proud of, the strides he'd made in the area of listening were especially gratifying. Sam also knew his wife would be the true judge of that, and he planned to ask Linda that night at dinner.

The next portion of the assignment asked him to describe his coaching success with Nick. For a second, he recalled the Nick that had banged out of his office the first time they met about Jerry's replacement. Nick's transformation since then was nothing short of amazing. Sam listed all the happy byproducts from their coaching relationship. The warehouse was now neat, clean, and well stocked. Orders were going out. Morale was way up. Costs, errors, and dealer complaints were significantly down. And Reggie wanted to roll out their process improvement to every warehouse in the region. If that wasn't success, Sam thought, what was?

He knew one important acid test remained—whether the program could be sustained. Still, it was worth a moment of elation. They were well on their way.

Sam didn't forget. That night, as they lingered at the table after dinner, he told Linda about the self-evaluation he'd done earlier in the day. "It seems like my listening skills are improving," he began tentatively, "but whatever the guide says, you're my real test."

Linda folded her napkin in perfect quarters and then broke into a broad smile. "Of course I agree—and it's not just your listening, it's everything!" she said emphatically, putting her arm around his shoulders and pecking his cheek with a playful kiss. "You've been so focused on Nick, telling me about how he's grown and all that he's accomplished. But I wish you could see yourself, Sam. I wish you could see what I see." And there it was: honest praise from his mate, better than any gold.

Nick arrived the next day for their coaching session wearing a curious smile that signaled Sam he had something up his sleeve. When they were seated, Sam said, "Okay, superstar, you hit the magic number. We made our goal. So where do we go from here?"

"Good question!" Nick fired back mischievously. "Wait till you hear this. We've been wrestling with how to keep this thing going, throwing a lot of ideas out there. We agreed to sleep on it. Then yesterday, Craig comes in and says he talked to his team, and they want to challenge Mike's team and mine to see which team can hit 100 percent fulfillment first, and then who can keep it up there the longest."

Sam was getting used to being dumbstruck in these situations. Still, the surprise and pleasure were evident on his face. Eight weeks earlier, they couldn't even hit the modest goals that were set for them. Today, they were talking about 100 percent fulfillment. Moreover, in all his years at the warehouse, Sam couldn't remember a single day when they'd reached 100 percent. Yet today, here they were, talking not only about hitting the high mark but also about sustaining it indefinitely.

Still, Sam was curious how they would sustain it. Weekly pizza wasn't feasible; some other reward would have to take its place.

Reading his mind, Nick moved ahead. "We're still working on the incentive piece. Our small groups came back to us with ideas, but there are some issues that need to get unkinked. They're retooling it now and will get back to us by next week. Meanwhile, everybody's pumped up about the competition. We're seeing these guys grow into real teams now."

Just like the Rams and the Bears, Sam thought. But he kept the thought to himself.

Sam watched the numbers for the next two days. Monday's and Tuesday's reports still showed gains, albeit in smaller increments. Things were moving up by half percentage points now, but they were still moving up.

The plan to network with other warehouses was beginning to work. A friendship Mike had with a supervisor at the Fairfield warehouse jump-started the effort. In short order, their contacts expanded to two additional warehouses in the region. Mike developed a system for rapidly flagging the back-ordered parts and contacting their partners at the other warehouses. When their partners shipped the part, they shot the FedEx tracking number back to Mike's team so the shipping checkers could record the dealer order as complete.

Sam's innate skepticism had in large part melted away. Lately, most of the things he'd thought were too much to hope for had in fact come to pass. However, he still wondered if they could actually get to 100 percent.

Early on Thursday, he took a deep breath and looked at Wednesday's lines-per-man-hour report. What he saw amazed him—all three teams had hit the 100 percent fulfillment mark. They'd done it! Sam punched the Print key and hurried downstairs to the time clock.

Nick, Mike, and Craig were all waiting by the board, along with a dozen or so warehouse guys. The murmur of conversation abruptly ceased at the sight of Sam practically running in their direction. This time he couldn't be coy with Nick. And, as Linda sometimes reminded him, he'd never had much of a poker face anyway. He held out the sheet of paper.

Nick studied it for less than a second, then let out a whoop that would have been the envy of any diehard fan—Rams, Bears, or otherwise. Quickly the report was passed to Craig and then to Mike, who let out similar whoops. Now everybody was cheering as more workers gathered to see what the hubbub was about.

Sam turned to go. This was their victory, after all. Nick, Craig, and Mike deserved the glory, and he would leave them to it. Almost to the stairway, he heard the sound of someone running to catch up with him. Nick stopped directly in front of him, blocking the way to the stairs.

"Where are you going?" Nick asked. "Aren't you going to celebrate with us?"

Sam heard music starting up in the background. Someone had put on Queen's "We Are the Champions" and was cranking up the volume. "Listen," Sam began, "This is your party, Nick. You made this happen. I'm just the lucky boss who got a talented guy like you to coach. Go back and enjoy it."

Sam sidestepped Nick and headed for the stairs, but Nick caught his arm. "What do you mean?" he demanded. "You did everything, Sam. Don't you remember how I used to be? Afraid of my own shadow until you helped me find my power? You showed me things I could do that I never thought were possible for me. You made this happen every bit as much as me." Nick's voice had become choked with emotion. He locked Sam in his gaze, and the two stood motionless as the song blared.

Finally, Sam spoke. "Yeah, I guess we're a pretty good team, huh?"

Nick nodded and then stopped abruptly. "Okay," he said with mock disapproval, "this was a perfect moment until you started up with that sports talk again." They both laughed. Together, they strolled back in the direction of the noise.

Later, in his office, Sam put a few final touches on his learning assignment. It hit him as he dialed in to join the conference call that this was the last one. *I guess I'm on my own after this*, he thought. Realistically, he knew he still had more to learn. He'd had some successes, but how would he handle coaching all his direct reports? That could be quite a juggling act.

Still, he felt good. He knew the fundamentals now. And one thing was certain: he'd have plenty of opportunities to practice.

"We've got a different format today," Scott announced. "For our last session, you each have five minutes to share your *Coaching to Win* experience with the group. Be sure you include any successes you'd attribute to having participated in this program."

The line went quiet, and Sam could feel the energy as he and the other guys mentally assembled their stories. It was daunting. Sam wondered how he could sum it all up in five minutes. So much had happened. *Stick to the high points,* he counseled himself. *No need to cover every last detail.*

Scott called names at random; Sam's was third on the list. He took a deep breath and began to tell the story of Nick's process improvement, how they had challenged themselves to make their percentage improvement goal. Sam recounted the meeting with all his supervisors, and how they brought to him not only a problem but a workable solution that had helped them achieve 100 percent fulfillment for the first time in the history of the warehouse. He laid out the facts and events simply and without drama. But when he came to the end, there was a burst of applause from his colleagues.

His five minutes were up, but Sam couldn't resist trying to squeeze in one more point. Asking Scott for another minute, he went on. "I can tell you the numbers we hit, but it's really about more than that. There's a whole new feeling in the warehouse. I see guys who have been with us fifteen or twenty years showing up for their shifts with smiles on their faces. They feel like they're part of something now—something we've only just scratched the surface of. In the end, that gets us something lots bigger than cost savings and dealer satisfaction."

When everyone had taken their turns, Scott was ready to turn them loose. "Don't think of this as being over," he advised. "The weekly calls are done, but for all of you, the bigger part of this is just starting. Use your contact list. Stay in touch with each other. Share your wins and encourage each other. I mean it sincerely—the best is yet to come."

After the call ended, Sam sat for a while. Highlights of the past eight weeks played in his mind like a movie trailer. As yet, the movie didn't have an ending. He was convinced, however, that he could help write a pretty good one.

Scott was right. There was work to do. Lois, the new warehouse supervisor, would start on Monday. And the project was far from over. They'd proved they could achieve 100 percent fulfillment, but for how long?

Questions for Nick were forming in his mind, but they could wait until next week. One thing was sure. Somewhere, in another part of the warehouse, Nick was already working things out.

Your Turn to Win: Feedback is the primary tool used in reinforcement and redirection.

1. Positive Feedback

- *Description:* Positive remarks either spoken or written that reinforce or recognize positive behaviors
- *Outcomes:* Reinforces and encourages desired behaviors

2. Constructive Feedback

- *Description:* Redirects others by helping them understand how to improve a behavior or attitude
- *Outcomes:* Reinforces and encourages desired behaviors

3. No Feedback

- *Description:* Nothing is said or done; no feedback is provided
- *Outcomes:* Colleagues make their own assumptions about their performance; outcomes are left to chance

1. Giving effective feedback is a foundational coaching skill. Giving positive feedback works well when it is prompt, sincere, and specific. Giving consistent reinforcement and recognition has been known to lead to the following benefits:

- increase in personal self-worth
- reduced stress
- improved morale
- increased job satisfaction
- strengthened performance

To really master the art of giving positive reinforcement, a leader must get in the *habit* of looking for opportunities to give genuine positive feedback. What types of things will you be watching for that will allow you an opportunity to provide positive feedback?

2. Some helpful reminders when giving constructive feedback or redirection are to

- share what is working well;
- identify specifically what needs to be changed or improved;
- describe the behaviors or attitudes needed;
- clarify and agree on future direction; and
- affirm your belief in your coachee's ability to achieve the goal and be successful.

Ideally, a leader would use constructive feedback less often than positive feedback. What will you watch for that will tell you your coachee is off track and would benefit from constructive feedback or redirection?

Chapter Ten
VICTORY LAP

Monday, 8:45 a.m.

A curious habit had been creeping into Sam's behavior. As he sat at his desk Monday morning, he caught himself humming. He couldn't name the tune—perhaps snatches of something he'd heard down in the warehouse. Whatever the reason, it seemed right.

And things certainly had been humming in the warehouse. It hardly seemed possible that Lois, Jerry's replacement, had been on board for two weeks now. Time would tell, but so far she was blending well with the team. Sam recalled that it wasn't so long ago that he believed he'd never find another "Jerry." However, finding Lois had proven him wrong, and Nick's rise showed there was talent all around him, waiting to be mined. For a guy who preferred to be proven right, he couldn't be happier with the way things were turning out.

Scrolling through Monday's e-mail, he clicked open a message from Reggie. Reggie wanted to meet tomorrow to do a wrap-up on Sam's *Coaching to Win* experience. There was much to talk about, Sam thought. The fulfillment numbers continued at 100 percent; each supervisor worked constantly with both the warehouse guys and the shipping checkers to keep it that way. And the pressure was on. Pride dictated that nobody wanted to be on the first team to fall below the century mark. Nick had told Sam that there would be a reward for the unfortunate team who let things drop below 100 percent. He didn't give details. He merely said that it involved large quantities of cold water.

Reggie had suggested they meet at the Downtown Café, the spot where all of this had begun. Tuesday morning, while the sun was still coming up, Sam slid into the booth opposite his boss. He ordered coffee and, on a whim, the French toast. Two pieces of Texas toast dipped in egg custard, grilled, and served with powdered sugar and choice of bacon, sausage, or ham. He was surprised how much easier it was for him to try new things now.

And he could afford the calories. Sam had gone down two waist sizes. Linda was taking him pants shopping that weekend. Or, as she told him, "Only the kids wear 'em that baggy."

The men made small talk until their orders arrived. Football season was a ways off, but they still managed to exchange some news about the Bears and Rams. As they ate, Reggie encouraged Sam to talk about his coaching experience over the eight weeks. Sam modeled his speech after the one he'd given to his colleagues on the final conference call with Scott, adding in all that had happened since. After working to improve his own listening skills, it felt good to be listened to.

Reggie heard Sam with a mix of pride and admiration. He was proud that he'd had a hand in getting this whole thing rolling, and admired how well Sam had followed through. Inside, he couldn't wait to roll out the process improvement to the other warehouses in the region. News of their 100 percent fulfillment achievement had quickly traveled to Reggie's superiors, and now there was pressure from on high to replicate all this on a much bigger scale. Still, there were lots of moving parts, and Reggie needed to make sure everybody was on board and a workable plan was in place.

Reggie posed the question. "You know I've been chomping at the bit to roll this thing out to our other warehouses. And I'm getting pushed by the guys upstairs to make it happen. But I really need your take—are we ready?"

"I think we're close," Sam responded. "I've talked to Nick about it. He's agreed to work with his counterparts in the other warehouses and to share what we learned in our process. That knowledge-sharing should spare them from making the same mistakes we did. Here's the other thing, though. I think we have to be careful about trying to make this thing cookie-cutter. Remember how you started it with me? 'People are more likely to support that which they help create.' We need to give each of these warehouses the opportunity to contribute their own ideas, to help create something that will work best for them. The timing is great. Now that Lois is getting up to speed, it will free Nick to help coordinate the whole thing."

Reggie smiled broadly. It was exactly what he'd hoped to hear. He was also curious about something else. "You know me, Sam—I always like to put a dollar sign to things. Do you think you can quantify the value of your *Coaching to Win* experience?"

Sam thought for a minute. At first it seemed like a funny question because he hadn't given it much thought in those terms. But the more he thought about it, the more it made sense.

"Yeah, I actually can!" Sam replied enthusiastically. "Year to date, our operating costs are down by over forty thousand dollars. About 75 percent of that is what we're saving on boxes and shipping costs alone. The rest has been in reduced restocking, less overtime, and some other stuff. Oh, something else—we had a guy retire last week, and the team decided not to replace him. They just absorbed his workload and made it part of their zones.

"I have got to hand it to Mike's guys. They solved the problem as a team. He told me there'd been some concern. With things running better now and them getting finished up early most days, they were worrying about layoffs. So they saw this guy retiring as a way to adjust the workload and reduce the chance that anybody on the team would be laid off in the future."

Reggie's look was intent as he listened. Sam could see him multiplying in his head the cost savings times the number of warehouses in their region. It was a pretty big chunk of change, and it had all happened in less than ten weeks.

And Sam's tale about Mike's guys was astounding. It was such a different scenario from what usually happened. They could easily have initiated a slowdown to force Mike to backfill the vacant position. Instead, they'd seen it as an opportunity to reinforce their own job security. The whole conversation was changing.

"Well, you know I'm anxious for a lot of reasons to get this going," Reggie admitted. "How long before we start talking to the other warehouses about getting on board?"

Sam smiled. He and Reggie were very much alike. In his shoes, Sam would be pushing the very same question. "Oh, we're ready now." Reggie looked surprised. "I do have a couple of questions, however. How many of the other warehouse managers have been through *Coaching to Win*? The reason our process improvement worked in the first place is because I learned a whole new set of skills for coaching my supervisors. Without that training, none of this could have happened. It's not something that comes naturally for me, but I was able to learn it in pretty short order."

Reggie mulled Sam's statement over. He was dead right. And the cost of putting those other managers through the program was small against the cost savings they were already reaping.

"Nick and I talked about it," Sam went on. "What we see happening is this. Those other managers go through *Coaching to Win*. They use the same objective we did and choose one of their supervisors to lead the project, just like I chose Nick. Nick picks it up at that point and works to engage that supervisor and their warehouse crew. Our experience here taught us you can't just change up the routine and expect everybody to automatically get on the bus. There has to be collaboration and an opportunity for each supervisor and each team to contribute in their own way."

As Sam laid out the plan, Reggie took notes. Sam suspected that the other plant managers hadn't been through *Coaching to Win* yet. But he knew Reggie was fired up to get things moving. He'd get those guys enrolled in the next session without fail.

Reggie finished writing and looked up. "Sounds like we're ready to pull the trigger on this thing," he said with satisfaction. "Anything else you need?"

Sam smiled. "Just your undying support," he shot back, and the men laughed. This game was about to move from the local sandlot to Yankee Stadium. The players were pumped and ready to go.

When Sam arrived back at the warehouse, he saw Reggie in conversation with Nick and the other supervisors outside the lunchroom. He was curious what they were talking about but resisted the impulse to join them. He needed to prepare for his second coaching session with Craig. Sam was discovering in their sessions what a talented communicator Craig was—another potential superstar on his team. He thought about how each of these guys had unique abilities. When those abilities were uncovered and applied to a set of goals, the effect on the business would be powerful.

Sam had just sat down with his field guide when Reggie appeared at the door. A manila envelope was in his hand. "Do I owe you for breakfast?" Sam joked.

Reggie chuckled. "No," he said, "but I forgot to give you this." He handed Sam the envelope and watched as Sam's hand slid inside and pulled out a certificate. "Congratulations, Sam," Reggie announced. "You've successfully completed *Coaching to Win*."

Sam's face flushed with pride as he gazed at the document. He'd never made a show of his own accomplishments. Certificates and diplomas did not cover his office walls. He kept them boxed on a shelf in the upstairs hall closet. But this one was a keeper. He'd ask Linda to help him select a frame, and he would choose a prime spot on the wall. It would remind him of the experience and of how, when he acquired the right tools, problems had turned into possibilities.

Sam's musing was interrupted by the sound of applause. Nick, Craig, Mike, and Lois had appeared behind Reggie in the doorway. He found himself blushing again. Lois stepped forward, her smartphone poised. "This is worth a photo," she declared. Sam obliged by holding up his certificate and giving a broad grin. That brought on another round of applause.

Silence followed, and then Sam spoke. "You don't know how much this means," he began, noticing the waver in his voice. "But I should really be clapping for you." All eyes were on him as he continued. "Yeah, I had a hand in this, but it's the talent that each of you bring in the door with you every day that makes it all work. To see all you grow, that's the gift for me."

Another moment of silence followed before Nick jumped in. "Thanks, Sam, and we're going to tiptoe out before you have us all bawling. There's work to be done! Go Rams! Go Bears!" As they filed out, strains of music filtered down the hall and through Sam's open door. The heavy metal guys had won the toss today.

That evening, Sam took a different route home from work. The route took him along Fairview Avenue, by the first home he and Linda had purchased when they came to town. *So much water had gone under the bridge since then,* he thought. The kids were grown. Retirement was a stone's throw away. Before *Coaching to Win*, Sam had been counting the days until he could hang it up.

Today, though, he was having a different thought. He wondered if he might put it off a couple of years. "The benefits are much better if I wait until I'm sixty-seven," he said to himself. He knew, however, that it was just an excuse. The real reason to stick around was that he was finally having fun—more fun than he'd ever had in his life.

He stopped in front of the old house and switched off the engine. The place had held up pretty well. A monarch butterfly flew down and rested on the polished hood of the car. It would be autumn soon.

Sam patted his jacket pocket. It contained a packet with tickets for a week in Aruba. Linda would be surprised.

The sky was incredibly blue. Sam looked out as if he were seeing it for the first time. His heart was light. Too many wins to even count. So much gold. He started the car again and turned toward home.

Your Turn to Win: While this marks the end of your formal *Coaching to Win* learning experience, you have only just begun your learning journey. Here are some final thoughts to inspire you to continue refining your coaching skills.

> *Coaching is about inspiring, empowering and enabling people to live deeply in the future, while acting boldly in the present.*
> —Robert Hargrove, *Masterful Coaching*

> *Achievement comes to you when you are able to do great things for yourself. Success comes when you empower followers to do great things with you. Significance comes when you develop leaders to do great things for you. A legacy is created when you put your organization into the position to do great things without you!*
> —John Maxwell, *The 21 Irrefutable Laws of Leadership*

What will be your coaching legacy?

EPILOGUE

Thursday, 9:38 a.m.

It was a different drive in to work for Sam on this particular morning. Linda sat next to him in the passenger seat, dressed in a sleek navy suit with a single yellow rose pinned to her lapel. Sam wore no coat but had put on a tie. It was, after all, the day of his official retirement, and he wanted to go out looking sharp.

Things had continued to go well at the warehouse—so well, in fact, that he had delayed his retirement for a couple of years. Finally, however, he was hanging it up. At an auction the Saturday before, he'd purchased a lathe, a band saw, and a good chest of tools. He wanted the next chapter of his life to be about things he would make with his hands: a crib for their second grandchild, due in February; shelving for Linda's pantry; and a dozen other projects he had in mind.

They parked in a reserved spot near the warehouse's main entrance. A large "Congratulations, Sam!" sign was affixed to the inside of the door, painted in bright blue letters and embellished with patches of red glitter that caught the morning sun. Arm in arm, Sam and Linda walked down the hall toward the murmuring crowd. The supervisors, Reggie, and the entire warehouse crew were gathered at the time clock. The smell of freshly brewed coffee was in the air, and an enormous tray of snickerdoodles lay on a nearby table. Linda had entrusted her recipe to Nick's fiancée so that the transition would be complete. Now the ceremony could begin.

There were speeches, a lot of laughter, and a few tears. No gold watch—Sam wouldn't have wanted one anyway. The gold he cared about was standing all around him. Nick presented him with a small wrapped box that, upon being opened, contained his famous green marker. Laughter rose, followed by a bear hug between Sam and Nick and then the most thunderous applause the walls of that warehouse had ever heard.

When the whole thing was done, Sam and his bride walked back down the hall and out the door for the last time. The Bears rally song blared from the speakers. Sam laughed out loud. For him, something was ending. For the folks inside, it was only beginning. For once, he had no worry. The music would play on.

ACKNOWLEDGMENTS

To Jesus Christ
for giving me the desire and courage to write this book.

To my husband, Dan, and sons, Mike and Mark
(the three most important men in my life),
who inspired me when I fell into doubt, whose
life experience added truth to situations in
the book, and whose enthusiasm for
this adventure was contagious.

To Pat Woertz,
my coach, mentor, and friend, for all the years
of support, encouragement, and prodding to
think bigger and reach higher.

To Kevin Peterson,
who was instrumental in the creation of the
Coaching to Win *learning experience.*

To the Profitable Ideas Exchange (PIE) and our
Coaching to Win Executive Network members
for keeping the coaching
conversation going.

To Rob Vickery, Mark Faust, Scott Anderson,
and Mark Lanham,
who miraculously came into my world
during this journey, and without whose
encouragement and guidance
this book might never
have come to fruition.

To all my readers,
I sincerely hope you will use the coaching tools in this book
to achieve success for yourselves and all those you coach.

ABOUT THE AUTHOR

Jane Pierce is president of Pierce Development Group. She earned an undergraduate degree in organizational behavior and leadership from the University of San Francisco and an MBA from Millikin University. She currently resides in Anaheim, California, and also serves as a member of the board for the California Diversity Council.

Open Book Editions
A Berrett-Koehler Partner

Open Book Editions is a joint venture between Berrett-Koehler Publishers and Author Solutions, the market leader in self-publishing. There are many more aspiring authors who share Berrett-Koehler's mission than we can sustainably publish. To serve these authors, Open Book Editions offers a comprehensive self-publishing opportunity.

A Shared Mission

Open Book Editions welcomes authors who share the Berrett-Koehler mission—Creating a World That Works for All. We believe that to truly create a better world, action is needed at all levels—individual, organizational, and societal. At the individual level, our publications help people align their lives with their values and with their aspirations for a better world. At the organizational level, we promote progressive leadership and management practices, socially responsible approaches to business, and humane and effective organizations. At the societal level, we publish content that advances social and economic justice, shared prosperity, sustainability, and new solutions to national and global issues.

Open Book Editions represents a new way to further the BK mission and expand our community. We look forward to helping more authors challenge conventional thinking, introduce new ideas, and foster positive change.

For more information, see the Open Book Editions website:
http://www.iuniverse.com/Packages/OpenBookEditions.aspx

Join the BK Community! See exclusive author videos, join discussion groups, find out about upcoming events, read author blogs, and much more! http://bkcommunity.com/

Printed in the United States
By Bookmasters